C.B

Please renew/return this item by the last date shown.

So that your telephone call is charged at local rate, please call the numbers as set out below:

	From Area codes 01923 or 020:	From the rest of Herts:
Renewals:	01923 471373	01438 737373
Enquiries:	01923 471333	01438 737333
Minicom:	01923 471599	01438 737599

L32   www.hertsdirect.org

One for Every Sleeper

One for Every Sleeper

The Japanese Death Railway through Thailand

Jeffery English

ROBERT HALE · LONDON

© Jeffery English 1989
First published in Great Britain 1989

Robert Hale Limited
Clerkenwell House
Clerkenwell Green
London EC1R 0HT

British Library Cataloguing in Publication Data

English, Jeffery
One for every sleeper.
1. Thailand. Railways. Burma–Siam Railway.
Construction by Allied prisoners of war
I. Title
940.54′72′52

ISBN 0–7090–3864–X

Photoset in Palatino by
Derek Doyle & Associates, Mold, Clwyd.
Printed in Great Britain by
St Edmundsbury Press, Bury St Edmunds, Suffolk.
Bound by WBC Bookbinders Limited.

Contents

Illustrations

Preface

This is the story of 400 prisoners of war who were captured by the Japanese on the fall of Singapore. Three and a half years later, when the atomic bombs on Hiroshima and Nagasaki meant the end of the war, 136 of them were released – but the other 264 died in captivity.

After over a year of idleness but increasing boredom and hunger at Changi on Singapore Island, they were sent up country as one of the numerous working parties to help the Japanese with the construction of the railway through the jungles of Siam, to link Siam with Burma. Five months of working were followed by three months in a 'recuperation camp': but in those eight months nearly two out of every three died, from common starvation or from the delights of cholera, malaria, beri-beri, dysentery, or gangrene.

It was quite a long railway, but for every sleeper laid it cost the life of one POW or of one coolie – the natives drafted up from the rubber plantations of Malaya, when the Japs ran out of working POWs, the majority of whom had irritatingly died.

Eight short months seemed quite long at the time with two out of every three dead.

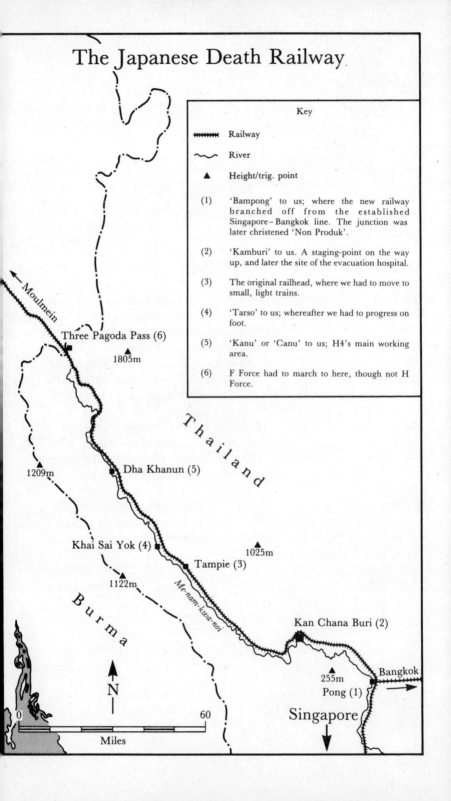

The Japanese Death Railway

Key

┼┼┼┼┼┼	Railway
∿	River
▲	Height/trig. point

(1)   'Bampong' to us; where the new railway branched off from the established Singapore–Bangkok line. The junction was later christened 'Non Produk'.

(2)   'Kamburi' to us. A staging-point on the way up, and later the site of the evacuation hospital.

(3)   The original railhead, where we had to move to small, light trains.

(4)   'Tarso' to us; whereafter we had to progress on foot.

(5)   'Kanu' or 'Canu' to us; H4's main working area.

(6)   F Force had to march to here, though not H Force.

Moulmein

Three Pagoda Pass (6)

▲ 1805m

Thailand

▲ 1209m

Dha Khanun (5)

Khai Sai Yok (4)

▲ 1025m

Tampie (3)

Me-nam-kwa-noi

▲ 1122m

Burma

Kan Chana Buri (2)

▲ 255m

Pong (1)

Bangkok

N

Singapore

0   60

Miles

1   Into Captivity

Singapore had fallen.

That afternoon, a staff officer, accompanied by an interpreter, had gone out through the lines under a large white flag to Bukit Timah, a small hill just to the north of the city, to sign the unconditional surrender of the British to the invading Japanese forces, with the prime object, in the words of General Yamashita, 'to save the innocent civilian population from the horrors of an all-out assault on the city'.

He was, of course, quite rational. There were over a million civilians in the city – Malays, Chinese, Tamils, and whatever. They were already suffering, and the small British Army had no hope whatsoever of protecting them. It was not that we were short of men, or of guns, or of ammunition – we were short of water.

The city's water supply normally came in from the mainland over the causeway, feeding two small reservoirs on the Island: but the causeway had been blown up (by us) towards the end of the retreat down the Malaya mainland, and the Japs had now overrun the reservoirs as well. They had cut off all supplies of water to the city, and we had had none for five days.

No water meant no sanitation. In a hot climate, just 80 miles north of the Equator, the result was dramatic. Disease, in the form of dysentery and cholera, became no mere remote threat, but an immediate and dire certainty. Not merely for the innocent civilians, but for the British Army as well, as witness the Cathay Building.

We had a General Headquarters, but it only had one corps, and so 3rd Indian Corps was the effective Fighting Headquarters. I was in command of the 3rd Indian Corps Signals Regiment (or the rump of it as most of our troops had been siphoned off a fortnight previously to provide 'reserve infantry' because corps was short of fighting men), and our job was to run the communications for 3rd Corps.

Corps HQ had moved down to the centre of the city two weeks earlier, with a not very happy choice of location. The Cathay Building was brand new, and was the highest skyscraper in the city, and corps established itself on the second and third floors. This despite loud protests from the Australian Division, who were already using the ground and first floors as their base hospital, and didn't like a fighting HQ moving into the same building with their Red Cross flag flying from the roof. Nevertheless, corps moved in, and the Red Cross flag continued to fly.

Now, this skyscraper housed over a thousand souls and after five days without any water, the whole place stank to high Heaven. Every loo had been used over and over again, but there was no water with which to flush them. It was no good saying 'get a bucket of water', because there was nowhere to fill a bucket. A thousand sets of bowels and a thousand bladders crying out for relief were causing the situation to deteriorate hourly, and the Cathay was no longer a very nice place to be.

There had been a lot of fine talk back in London about Singapore being defended 'to the last man, and to the last round', but we didn't surrender because of lack of men or of ammunition – we surrendered because of lack of water, for the million civilians as much as for the Army. The finest military equipment in the world won't help you if you are unwashed, dirty, smelly, and above all dehydrated. Anyway, we were thirsty, and we capitulated.

It was an eerily quiet evening and night after the white flag party had gone out, and the firing gradually died down and then eventually petered out.

We had been told to quit our operational positions and to return to our billets or sleeping areas, which for my little

unit meant leaving the Cathay and going to the museum
300 yards away where our off-duty personnel slept and
ate. Fortunately, the museum was surrounded by lawns
and flowerbeds, and so we had been able to dig latrines
which came as a great relief, in all senses of the word,
particularly to those who had been cooped up in the
stench of the Cathay.

We waited all night, and at about 9 a.m. the Japs moved
in. They came in by the lorry-load, all standing up and
clutching little paper Jap flags – a large red dot on a white
background, known to them as the *Rising Sun* but to us as
the *Poached Egg*.

They showed no sign of emotion whatsoever. Had it
been the victorious British entering a conquered city, the
troops would have been waving their flags and shouting
and singing (and most of them at least half drunk): but the
Japs stared steadfastly forward, without uttering a sound,
and not even waving their little flags. They took not the
slightest notice of us waiting by the roadside. It was even
more eerie. Mark you, as we later learnt, when they got
past us and down into the Chinese native quarter, things
were different, and within twenty-four hours there was
not a virgin to be found amongst the one million
population.

We stayed where we were, and very soon got some
preliminary orders. There were to be no separate officer
camps and other rank camps, as there were in Germany.
Officers would stay with their men, and whole units
would stay together, with one important exception: we
would be separated into 'Whites' and 'non-Whites'.

I would explain that the official name of 'Corps' was
'3rd Indian Corps', and that the two original divisions
were both Indian Divisions. In each Indian Division you
had two brigades, each with two Indian Battalions and
one British Battalion. The Indian Battalions had mostly
white officers – but all of the soldiery were Indians.
Specialist troops like Engineers and Signals were
all-white.

In addition to the two original divisions, we had the
Australians, who were naturally all-white; and the poor
wretched 18th Division, which had only arrived in Malaya

from England as we were scampering back over the causeway, and the campaign was nearly over. Furthermore, by some superb piece of administrative planning, whilst the troops themselves were landed at Singapore, all their artillery and armoured troop carriers had been sent to Java, and so, armed with little else but their rifles, most of the 18th Division walked off their ships and almost immediately into the bag, with three and a half years in prison camps ahead of them.

All in all, there were a lot of Indians, but there were still more Whites, including the Australians and the 18th Division. Approximately 47,000 non-Whites, and 53,000 Whites, so roughly 100,000 altogether.

The Japs were at a loss – there were more of us than they had expected. They separated us by colour, not having heard of 'racial discrimination' or of 'the rights of ethnic minorities', and we were to go to two huge camps, the Whites to Changi, and the non-Whites to Farrer Park.

Whilst we were waiting at the museum, they had mercifully restored the mains water. We heard rumblings in the pipes, and when the taps were turned on, through them came water, at first brownish but suitable for washing and sanitation, but rapidly becoming crystal clear. We boiled it before drinking it, but could scarcely wait for it to cool before gulping it down. Manna from Heaven had nothing on this. You can go for some while without eating, but 80 miles north of the Equator you cannot last for very long without water. It was sheer bliss.

However, on the third day we were to march.

As 'Whites', we were to go to Changi, on foot. Small units were to collaborate, but we could have one lorry for every thousand men to carry the cooking equipment and rations for ten days, whilst everything else – spare clothing, bedding, personal belongings and so on – would have to be carried by the individuals.

Changi was only 17 miles away, but when we came to do it, it felt much further.

We passed through the little village 5 miles out from the city, which had been Corps HQ only two weeks earlier but was now just a heap of still-smouldering ruins, there having been no water to put out the flames when it was bombed: there was a very nasty smell from the heap of corpses by the side of the large communal grave still being dug. We pressed on.

We got to Changi.

The whole area of Changi comprises a 6-square-mile promontory bounded on three sides by the sea. It supported the famous Changi Gaol, a modern but forbidding edifice modelled, so we were told, on America's equally famous Sing-Sing: further on there were four separate barrack complexes, each about a mile apart and each designed to house a battalion of about 900 men. Each had a central Barrack Square, flanked with three major buildings on each of the long sides (Barrack 'Squares' tend to be oblong rather than square), and a seventh on the short side at one end. There were then sundry small houses round about, which had served as married quarters. Four 900-man complexes, a total of 3,600: and now 53,000 of us moved into them. They suddenly seemed to be rather less spacious, and the amenities were sadly lacking.

There was no running water (which meant no sanitation), no electricity, no gas, and no fuel of any kind, which meant no means of cooking. But there were thousands of unexploded shells lying around from a magazine which had blown up during the battle; there were bomb craters everywhere; masses of barbed wire, telephone wires, and formerly overhead power-cables cluttering up the roadways; and many of the buildings had received direct hits. It was a shambles – but a fair-sized shambles – and most of us got ourselves under at least some sort of cover.

My own little unit spent the first night divided between two bathrooms and a billiards room in a married quarter (the billiards table was still there): but on the following morning we were moved out and given the whole bottom floor of a complete house which had been a married quarter. It even had a gramophone and a few unbroken records: but our immediate job was not to listen to gramophones, but to organize a cook-house and to dig ourselves latrines – which was where the trouble started.

All over Changi, every unit was doing likewise.

Hundreds of cook-houses. Hundreds of latrines. Nothing to make the cook-houses fly-proof. Nothing to cover up the open trench latrines. In the twinkling of an eye, millions of flies arrived – and with them arrived dysentery. Dysentery, in case you don't know, is a violent form of tummy trouble and diarrhoea, which doesn't go away. The flies, revoltingly enough, spread it by walking about in the latrines used by a sufferer, and then, without wiping their feet, walking about on your food. You eat the food – and you've got dysentery too. It took us several days to get organized – but the flies got organized immediately, and dysentery soon got a grip on Changi from which it never subsequently shook itself entirely free.

Our immediate priority was water. The Royal Engineers had managed to get one stand-pipe going about 200 yards away from us, but it was not a very strong flow and we were rationed to one water-bottleful per man per day. Half of that was impounded for the cook-house, and the other half you could drink, so the only hope for getting ourselves clean was the sea, to which we fortunately were tolerably near. We took the opportunity with gusto.

We got cleaner. We got the camp cleaner. We cleared up the wire, we filled in the bomb holes, we gathered up the unexploded shells, and we gradually got ourselves organized. As the days went by the REs got several more taps and stand-pipes working. But we still had no running water sanitation, and those open latrines became more and more worrying. We heard rumours that several neighbouring units had already developed cases of dysentery, although we ourselves were still mercifully free. There was no possibility of stopping the flies themselves from becoming contaminated, but there *was* the possibility of making the cook-house itself reasonably fly-proof.

There was no wire gauze about, and one could not just ring up a shop and have some delivered: so I called my officers together and told them that one of us would have to give up his mosquito-net for the good of the community, and we cut a pack of cards to see who should have the privilege and honour.

It wasn't a pleasant sacrifice to call upon anyone to make, for although Changi itself was still at this time remarkably free from malaria, we all imagined naturally that Changi was merely a stop-gap, and that once the Japs had made arrangements for permanent POW camps, we should be moved either to Japan or over onto the mainland – where to sleep without a net would mean almost inevitable malarial infection.

However, better that one of us should get a dose of malaria later than that all of us should get dysentery now: so we cut the pack of cards amongst us and a comparative newcomer to the unit called 'Goldie' drew the one which put the rest of our most uneasy minds at rest.

We cut it up (his net – not the card), covered the windows and made a curtain over the door; and it did its stuff handsomely, for we in our unit didn't get a single case of dysentery from that cook-house although within days it was to break out with alarming rapidity all over Changi. But it wasn't until weeks later that I learnt the full irony of the position of the poor wretched Goldie. His father, back in Scotland, was of all things a mosquito-net manufacturer; so whilst the head of the family at home was churning them out by the thousands, his unfortunate son was watching his only one being tastefully draped around our cook-house.

Not that there was much to cook. We had no fresh meat or bread or vegetables, but only the traditional bully and biscuits, with some tinned pilchards, tinned vegetables, and cheese, and some cooking-oil. Our cooks made the most of it, producing bully and vegetable stew, fried bully rissoles, and so on, so that we had some hot meals if little in the way of variety.

The Japs had ordered us to bring in ten days of our own rations; and although we had brought in rather more, they were only reckoning on ten, and as from the eleventh day they started themselves to issue us with rations.

The scale consisted of a pound of rice a day, with nominal quantities of salt, tea, sugar, and oil: and that was that. No meat, no vegetables, no bread or even flour to make it with: so we decided to switch over as quickly as possible to the new scale, and to save what remained of our decent food to help us out for as long as it could.

At first, a whole pound of rice a day was far more than most of us could stomach, particularly as our cooks had no idea of how to cook it except by plain boiling. So, we limited ourselves to two meals a day, serving a plateful of boiled rice with a cheese sauce, half a pilchard, or one ounce of bully – a small tin between ten – helped out with two army biscuits with jam on the same generous scale. And starting with what seemed the enormous quantity of 4 ounces a day of rice (dry rice, of course, before cooking), by the end of a fortnight we'd worked our way up to the full pound and were ravenous for more.

We found an old oil-barrel, which we dug into a bank of earth with a space underneath for a fire, thereby making an oven. We got down to experimenting with the beastly stuff, tediously making rice flour by grinding it with a bottle on a concrete slab: but the results were discouraging, the biscuits that came forth when we tried to make a light pastry merely endangering the teeth.

Meanwhile the change of diet had given half of the unit acute constipation, whilst the other half were running around with equally violent diarrhoea. I had a horrible fear that the latter was the onset of dysentery, which by now was raging all around us: but Goldie's net continued to do its stuff, and our little unit remained free from the real scourge for another six months.

And so, for three weeks, we remained precisely as we were from that first morning. We were still in our original fighting formations, officers with their own men, units under their old Brigade Headquarters, brigades in divisions, and so forth: most of us scarcely ever even saw a Jap. The Japs sent their orders to Malaya Army Headquarters, HQ sent out orders to corps and divisions in the old way: and all the 'usual channels' functioned just as during the campaign, with the minimum of inconvenience and trouble to the Japs. In accordance with their instructions we had submitted nominal rolls of all still alive and in the camp: but that was as much as they knew about us, and they hadn't even come along and counted us for themselves.

At the end of three weeks, however, they decided to do

something about this: and they told us that instead of remaining in one large blob, we should sort ourselves out into five separate groups, and should build ourselves five separate prison camps.

'Five Camps' made sense.

There were the four major barrack complexes, but there was also a small collection of recently constructed wooden huts in a nearby rubber plantation. These had been put up since the start of the war to act as a staging camp for an Indian battalion: and although more than primitive, they represented 'accommodation' – and accommodation was at a premium.

Our people were split into five groups. One barrack complex was allocated to the Australians, who had always been something of a law unto themselves. One was allocated to the 18th British Division, who were more or less intact and had most of their men. One was allocated to the hospital, which was destined to require more and more space: and one was allocated to the 'Central Area' – GHQ and its innumerable auxiliary units. That left the wooden huts, which were given to the 9th/11th Division.

At the start of the campaign there had been two Indian Divisions up in the north guarding the Malaya/Thailand Border – the 9th and the 11th Divisions – and they had borne the brunt of the fighting. After a month of the retreat down the mainland they had become so decimated that they were amalgamated into the single '9th/11th Division', under a single command. After the Surrender, all of their Indian troops had gone off to Farrer Park – but we in Changi had all of their white officers, and all of their technical units such as their artillery and their engineers, who had white troops as well as white officers – and so the 11th Division (the 9th had been tacitly dropped) still comprised quite a few bodies, although not of a full divisional strength.

My own little unit was something of a floating kidney. Corps Headquarters did not really have any troops of its own, except mine: and so I was lumped in with the 11th Division and off we moved to the wooden huts.

2   An Extended Stay

It could have been worse. A number of huts had been burnt to the ground or generally smashed up during the bombing, but most of them were still standing. They were made of rough planking, with gaps for windows and doors (no actual doors, and no glazing or shutters) – but with the hot climate that didn't matter very much. What *did* matter was that the roofs were of the local variety of thatch, made from palm-fronds, and these were full of holes which let in the rain, which happened every evening. However, there were numerous palm-trees scattered around, and we were very quickly able to repair the damage.

For my two hundred men I was allotted two long huts, and the men, lying on the floor along either side, had 3 feet of headspace apiece, which was very much better than obtained in some of the other major barrack areas. For my seven officers, we got a little plate layers' hut up against the derelict railway which had served the coastal guns: 18 foot by 10, and infested (as we soon found out) with bed bugs. Ever tried bed bugs? They lurk in the crevices of the woodwork, and as soon as you pause to sit down, let alone go to sleep, they emerge for a feed. They live on blood, and although you might not begrudge them a smallish meal, they make you itch fiendishly. They made *us* itch. Nevertheless, that plate layers' hut was to become 'home' to us for the next three months, and when we came to leave it we did so almost with regret.

We then had to 'make ourselves a camp'. This consisted simply of putting up a barbed wire fence around a prescribed perimeter. It wasn't a very impressive fence – a row of 4-foot posts with wire criss-crossed and splayed out to pegs on either side: and at the two camp entrances from the main road we didn't run to gates – there were merely gaps in the wire. In fact, it was more of a boundary line than an obstacle – we'd been told to stay in, and that anyone found outside would be shot: but that was all.

'Getting out' thus at no time presented the slightest difficulty or problem. To the person whose mind dwells upon European prison camps, with their high walls, tall barbed-wire fences, searchlights, machine gun posts, sentries pacing up and down with fixed bayonets and fierce dogs whilst all the prisoners busily dig tunnels, this may pose the question as to why we didn't all escape. But escape to where? In Europe, once you got out, you might get away: but if *we* 'got out' then where on earth, literally, could we go to? India? Australia? In either case this meant 2,000 miles across waters patrolled proudly and triumphantly by the Jap Navy and by Jap aircraft, and dotted with islands with alert Jap garrisons. And where did you find a boat? A dhow or a junk were the limits of local possibilities, and the few that existed were each the treasured possession of some local native who would howl blue murder if it quietly disappeared in the night. And even if one stole one, where would one find the provisions and the compass and the water and even the pots to put the water in, sufficient for 2,000 miles? It just wasn't on.

One could, of course, walk. Still 2,000 miles, but of a different character, overland to India through Burma: part of it – the best part of half of it – over the mountains through trackless uninhabited jungle, where hacking one's way through at 2 miles a day would be remarkably good going, and absolutely devoid of food. As for the first part, the inhabited part, we couldn't forget that the population consisted entirely of Chinese, Tamils, and Malays. If you 'got away' in Europe, you didn't look too unlike the local populace to stir up speculation. But with little flat-nosed, fat brown Malays, thin Chinese with almond eyes and yellow skins, and even thinner jet-black Tamils averaging five-foot-nothing tall, what hope had you? With his big red face, big bony knees, wavy instead of crinkly hair, his probability of not knowing the language, and a nose the shape of nothing met with east of Rangoon, an Englishman had as much chance of appearing in public unnoticed as would a zebra in the Derby. Once again, it would have meant remaining hidden and undetected for months, and yet meanwhile eating. And as the only means of eating would be by stealing, it would scarcely have needed a bloodhound to follow a little trail of raided food-stores winding up through the 1,000 miles from Changi until one plunged into the jungle in Thailand. You *couldn't* escape. A few brave (or foolhardy) souls tried, but not one single one got through. Either they starved, got drowned, or were betrayed, tortured and shot. It wasn't on. And so the Japs, very sensibly and fully aware of this, at no time took the slightest precautions against our 'escaping' from our camps. If you got out, you'd either be back for your next meal or would get rounded up.

They were, however, quite genuinely concerned to see that we didn't get out amongst the local populace to stir up trouble or sabotage. It was therefore made an offence, punishable by death, to have any contact whatsoever with the natives. We all had our ring fences marking our inner camps, but a fence had also been constructed right across the base of the peninsular. This left a sort of no man's land all around us, known as the 'outer area'. We were allowed into the outer area in organized parties for such purposes as collecting firewood or taking sick men over to the hospital; and to show that you were an organized party, a flag had to be carried aloft on a stick by an officer leading a working party of any number of men, even though the Japs no longer had any means of identifying officers. The Japs had said that as we had surrendered we were no longer 'soldiers' but merely 'prisoners'. All ranks, Officers and NCOs alike, would therefore remove their badges of rank – crowns, pips, stripes, or what have you – and just become look-alike prisoners. That meant that even a British General was now deemed to be inferior to a private soldier of the Imperial Japanese Army, and when passing one, would have to salute him. If you passed him without saluting, you got a thump with his rifle butt, and were sent back to pass again: this time, crawling on your hands and knees. But, wearing badges of rank or not, the flag-bearing chap in charge of a working party failed to salute at his peril. Each camp had two flags, so that we could send out two working parties simultaneously – one, for instance, felling and chopping firewood. Whilst another could be drawing rations or ferrying sick men to the Central Hospital.

We only met the Japanese on working parties. Once the inner camps had been set up, the Japs didn't come inside – they were restricted to the outer area. In some ways, not surprisingly. They only put on fifty camp guards to guard 53,000 prisoners: but unless you went on a working party, most of us seldom if ever saw a Jap.

I shouldn't say 'Jap'. They had dropped the word 'Japan' wherever they could, and substituted 'Nippon'. Even the English language newspaper from Tokyo (which continued to be published) changed its name from *The Japanese Times* to *The Nipponese Times*: we found that if you called a Jap a Jap he would become infuriated, but that if you called him a 'Nip' he was perfectly happy. They became Nips; and to POWs and to ex-POWs 'Nips' they will forever remain.

The earliest and most pressing working parties required were those for collecting firewood. Wood was our only fuel for cooking (and rice needs to be cooked), and so every morning a flag was taken out, and any unit or regiment that wanted to send its own squad to join the party to bring in whatever it could find, could do so. For the first few weeks, it was largely a matter of prowling around and scrounging fallen trees and branches: but with firewood required at a 100 tons a day (that sounds a lot, but it's only 4 pounds a head between 50,000 men) these soon disappeared.

Something more permanent was required: and so all our best woodsmen were formed into a felling-party, and they went out felling trees every day all day and sawing them up into manageable loads. And then twice a week a hauling convoy went out and brought the timber in.

At first we'd started off with the nearest trees just

outside our inner camps, and managed with all sorts of little hand-carts and barrows and anything we could improvise to move anything too heavy to simply drag by ropes or too knobbly to roll. But as we got further and further away with the felling, some form of transport became essential. We asked the Nips for lorries, and they roared with merriment. Petrol for lorries for the prisoners? Nonsense. Finally they let us have a hundred derelict wrecks, and these we stripped down until each was just a bare chassis with wheels, brakes, and steering. We built flat wooden platforms onto each of them, fixed them up with ropes at the front, and with a motive power of up to twenty prisoners, we produced the 'Changi Trailers' which were to become our standard form of transport. They were used for everything – wood-hauling, ration-drawing, water-carrying, and hearses: and if you want to get slim, I can thoroughly recommend a stint of hauling a 2-ton load on a 1-ton 'Trailer' up a nice steep hill around noon just north of the Equator.

A more popular party soon came into being in the shape of the 'salt-water parties'. Our official ration of salt was so small that we found our rice almost inedible unless we cooked it in sea water. Now that we were confined to our inner camps we could no longer go for a bathe in the sea when it took our fancy: but an authorized outer area party going down to the sea had to wade out quite a way to get water which was clean enough for cooking and so got all of the bathing it wanted. Some people's appetite was ruined by the fact that the Nips, a little earlier, had lined up a hundred and fifty Chinamen 200 yards away along the beach from where we were allowed to go to get our water, machine-gunned them, and left them for us to bury: and now, as the tide kept coming in and going out each day, it kept uprooting bits of them, and odd arms or legs or sets of ribs sticking up out of the sand kept reminding us of them. However, the water for cooking was going to be boiled, so what?

These were 'internal working parties', to cope with our own needs: but within a month of our initial arrival the Nips started calling for working parties of prisoners for their own requirements.

The first to affect me was when they called upon the 11th Division to provide a hundred truck drivers and fitters, of which my own unit's quota was ten. As conditions at Changi were not all that salubrious, there was no shortage of volunteers; and off they went in the middle of March. They stayed away for a month. When they came back in April, their ardour had cooled. They'd been down in Singapore City, where they had found conditions even worse than at Changi, with long working hours and a lot of bashing about by the Nip NCOs. Their job had been to repair British lorries. Although they had patriotically done their stuff with iron filings in the sumps and half-cut-through brake cables, doing far more damage than good to the vehicles, the stories they told of beatings up and ill treatment had the obvious result: and when we had a demand for a new party of one officer and thirty men a week later, there were few volunteers.

As fortune would have it, this second party had the time of their lives, their job being to clear up the warehouses at the docks. Goldie (of the mosquito net) who'd gone in charge got a letter to me a week or so after they'd gone, through a man returning sick, and told me that they were very comfortably housed in 'The Great World', a huge former taxi-girl dance-hall-cum-brothel. They had real beds to sleep in, in the brothel area, and were feeding magnificently. He himself had even acquired a replacement mosquito net from the brothel store cupboard.

Their job was to move out the contents of the bomb damaged warehouses and to stack them on the quayside for the Nips to collect and remove to safer storage – and as nobody knew just what was inside the warehouses, the odd crate or two would never be missed. Their luck was that one of the damaged warehouses being evacuated contained British canned food. They were transported from the brothel down to the docks each day in a Nip lorry, and on the very first evening the spare tyre had been slashed around the inside and provided generous space to remove ample canned food for thirty men from the docks back to The Great World daily. The working party had no desire to come back to Changi.

The 'spare tyre' loading each day was organized by Goldie – but a little private enterprise also went on amongst the men. They were lined up before leaving the docks to be counted, and unduly bulging pockets were asking for trouble. Other means were found. Only one man got into real trouble. He was wearing an Australian style high domed bush hat; and at the vital moment when the Nip went by a sudden gust of wind blew it off, leaving him looking a little sheepish with three tins of sardines balanced on the top of his head. He lost his sardines, and was beaten up: but although everyone else was ordered to remove his hat, nobody else had been playing the 'Hat Trick' that evening (most of them only had flat hats) and the Nips looked no further.

Several months passed, and many more Nip working parties were called for. Increasingly, however, they weren't just for jobs down in Singapore City, but were described as 'overland parties'. Where they were bound for, the Nips didn't tell us – the parties just went off over the now-repaired causeway into Malaya, and rumour had it that proper hutted camps were being built up around Penang and Khota Baru – but this was only rumour. The Nips would demand large parties of 1,000, 2,000, or maybe only 500 at a time: and as far as possible we sent complete battalions or units with their own officers, cooks, and everything else. Men who were really sick were left behind: but six months after the Surrender we were down from our original 53,000 to less than half of that, with a high proportion of sick. My own little unit, having contributed towards the two 'Singapore working parties', was not called upon to send any men on the 'overland parties': but at the end of July we were detailed as a complete unit to go on an 'overseas party', which we were told was going to Japan.

There were to be two of these overseas parties, which the Nips themselves christened 'Japan Party A' and 'Japan Party B' – not 'Nip' or 'Nippon' Parties; and so in referring to them we reverted to the old lingo. 'Japan Party A' would consist of 1,000 mixed officers and men, whilst 'Japan Party B' would be only 500 strong, but would include all officers in Changi over the rank of

Lieutenant-Colonel, i.e. all of the full Colonels, the Brigadiers, and the five Generals. For the trip, we were all to be issued with special 'warm clothing', for none of us had anything other than tropical shirts and shorts, and most of us only had one each of those.

It was a curious collection which we got, consisting for each man of one thick shirt, a woolly vest, a pair of long pants, a cardigan, and either a scarf or a balaclava helmet. How we should have looked wearing the balaclava and cardigan, with long woolly pants sticking out from our tropical shorts and trickling dismally down into sockless boots, I shudder to think – but that's all we got, and after six months with our original clothes wearing thin, we felt lucky to be getting it.

Before they took the risk of letting us into their unspeakable country, however, the Nips wanted to make sure that we were not going to contaminate it; and so the day before our scheduled departure, we were all marched up onto the old gun park in the 18th Division Area for a medical inspection by the Nips' own MOs.

We arrived there at 10 a.m. to be ready by half-past; but we waited for six whole hours before the Nips showed up. And then we were tested to see if we had dysentery or malaria. The 'test' was the highlight of Nip medical sophistication, and consisted of what came to be known as 'glass-rodding'. We filed up before the Nip MOs, and then in full view of everyone else on the gun park, you dropped your trousers, bent over, and the Nip thrust a small glass rod up your posterior which provided them with a specimen for a microscope slide. Whether they ever got around to analysing the slides was somewhat doubtful (we were due to sail the following day), but to see their own officers thus dealt with before their very eyes brought enormous and ill-concealed pleasure to our own troops, and so maybe the exercise was not entirely wasted.

The Generals and Japan Party B were done first, and whilst this was happening one of my troops, having quickly seen what was in store, came up and urgently importuned me. 'It's the piles, Sir' he said. 'I've got 'em 'anging down like bunches of grapes. It'll kill me'. I saw his point immediately. So long as the Nips got their full

quota of slides for their filing-drawers, presumably they'd
be happy: so I selected a particularly nondescript-looking
man standing near the front of the queue, and told him
that after he'd been done he was to go round to the back of
the queue and then come up for a second prod. He didn't
relish the idea, but orders were still orders: and
meanwhile my grape-grower mingled with the crowd and
was spared.

A few days before this particular inspection a party of
prisoners from Java and Sumatra had come into Changi,
also, they had been told, *en route* for Japan. Both Java and
Sumatra (the core of the 'Dutch East Indies') had been
overrun by the Nips immediately after the fall of
Singapore: and although the majority of this new party
were Dutch, there was a sprinkling of British amongst
them.

They now came up onto the gun park with us for
glass-rodding (they were to be Japan Party C); and as they
marched in I caught a glimpse of an officer near the front
who looked vaguely familiar. He was wearing Dutch
Army clothes with a Dutch Army hat – but as he came
closer there could be no mistake, and I went over and
greeted my own former Colonel of 3rd Indian Corps
Signals. Although he had originally gone off with the
Front Line Infantry, he had been sent off to Java as a one
man advance party a few days before the end, when it was
thought that the war might be continued from there.

We sat down on a barrel swapping experiences, and he
told me that he had got onto one of the big liners which
left Singapore several days before the end, but that after
an exciting journey dodging bombers they had been
halted in the Sunda Straits by Japanese destroyers. The
ship had been duly sunk, but by some exceptional
oversight the lifeboats had not been machine-gunned (as
was the Jap custom), and they had managed to get ashore.
He had spent a month on Banka Island before being
moved to a big Dutch camp at Palembang on the mainland
of Sumatra, never reaching Java at all.

A whole lot of ships had met their doom in the same
way and in the same vicinity as had his. Unescorted and
unarmed (we hadn't got a Navy in the Far East since the

sinking of *Repulse* and the *Prince of Wales*), they had been entirely helpless when confronted by the Japanese warships, and numerous mutual friends had last been seen swimming in the water but had not been heard of since. Not only had survivors in lifeboats or swimming in the water usually been shot up from the destroyers, but one batch at least – a party of Australian women nurses from one of the hospitals – had struggled ashore but were prevented from landing by the Nip troops on the beach. The Nips waved them away, and tried to make them swim away again: and when the nurses took no heed (never dreaming that the Nips meant it), they had calmly opened up with tommy-guns and mowed them down in the surf. They had then come along and bayonetted any of those still wriggling: but one woman, stabbed through the breast, swooned and was left for dead. It was she who, after being found and cared for by some natives, was later brought to one of the camps and was able to tell her horrible story.

Our reminiscences were interrupted by the arrival of the Nip MOs for the glass-rodding exhibition: and when it was all over we went back to our respective inner camps to get ready for the move tomorrow.

No orders had as yet come as to the timing for tomorrow's move, but we cooked up some fried rice rissoles as a haversack ration, and packed our scanty belongings in readiness for the move. We slept on our baggage, and the next morning patiently sat on it just inside the gate, expecting an order at any moment to up sticks and march off to the lorries.

By lunch time nothing had happened, so at last we ate our rissoles, and as evening approached we got some friendly cooks from a neighbouring unit who were not involved to cook us some more rice for our evening meal.

Enquiries had been made to the Nips several times during the day, but each time they simply told us to stand by at one hour's notice – and at one hour's notice we remained for the rest of the week, never knowing whether the meal being cooked would be eaten, and not daring to wash our clothes or start anything else that couldn't be dropped immediately should the movement order come.

Instructions had been issued as to the procedure at the docks, whereby our packs would all be fumigated, our haversacks and mess gear sprayed, and we ourselves would have to strip and go through a bath of disinfectant, all of our clothes being fumigated whilst we personally were in the sheep-dip.

They also had the insolence to issue each of us with a printed circular which warned us of heavy import duties on any furs, jewellery, perfumes, and liquor taken into Japan; and in extra heavy type we were advised that there was an absolute ban on pornographic literature or dirty photographs.

Apart from the fact that we were singularly deficient in fur coats and tiaras, our only perfume for months had been that which Lifebuoy Soap claims so adequately to prevent; and in any event we hadn't the slightest desire to go anywhere near their beastly little country. It seemed a trifle hard if we were to be soaked for Customs Duty every time our captors chose to shift us across their measly frontiers, and the principle rankled even if we'd nothing on which we could possibly pay. The slur on our moral characters, too, contained in the reference to low-down literature was all the more keenly resented in that we hadn't seen any for months.

Still we stood by, and at last an order came through that Japan Party B, containing the Generals, would go at the end of the week: but although we made daily enquiries from the Nips, still no orders came for moving Japan Party A.

Nothing more was ever heard of Japan Party A. We stayed at one hour's notice for weeks until it quietly petered out, never being officially cancelled, but merely sinking into oblivion as everyone gradually lost interest. But meanwhile something else happened in which we were very interested indeed.

Nothing that the Nips had done to us during those first five months had been particularly dreadful. We were ill-housed, ill-clothed, ill-fed, and frequently humiliated: but we were surviving and had made the best of our lot as we could.

We had rapidly mended our roofs, and made our huts

water-tight. Our Royal Engineers had ferreted out the entire water supply system, and we now had running water wherever needed, in the cook-houses and at the ablution points. For the first couple of months our only lighting after dark had been from small oil lamps made possible by the discovery of a number of drums of kerosene in one of the derelict gun emplacements, although the camp was fully wired up with most of the light bulbs still intact – but we had no mains supply.

The Nips only patrolled the outer area, and didn't seem to be interested in what we did in the inner camps – and they only patrolled by day and slept in their guard room at night. One night, a party of our Engineers went out through the gate, unchallenged, dug up the main road, connected up a spur from the mains cable, ran it back into our camp and re-laid the main road surface. We had light throughout the camp – and the Nips either didn't notice (they were only around in daylight), or simply didn't *want* to notice. They wanted the quiet life.

This came as a particular boon to my unit.

When you are cut off from the world, and living only for the day when your compatriots will come and rescue you, 'news' from outside becomes most precious.

When we first came to Changi, it had been bombed, but it hadn't been looted: numerous wireless sets had been found and either kept or used for their components to make other sets. Anyone who had found one had probably still got it and was operating it (if he had batteries or electric power); and we got nervous in case the Nips sent up some sort of GPO detector van and found some. They had made it crystal clear that the radios were absolutely forbidden, with the usual threat of the death penalty for anybody found with one: so the order was issued that all 'private' radios would have to be moth-balled, and that just one 'official' set would be operated in each inner camp. The Royal Corps of Signals naturally took on the responsibility, and so the 11th Division camp set was operated by the 11th Division Signal Regiment. However, as the 11th Divisional Signal Regiment had been an early candidate for an overland working party, the doubtful privilege was handed over to my little Corps Signals.

It was a prettily designed little set. There was always the chance of a Nip search, and so the set was suitably disguised. Two old lorry accumulators were wired together, linked to a pathetic little string of half a dozen 12-volt bulbs which 'lighted' one end of one hut. One of the accumulators was just what it looked like – it was the battery which provided the electricity. The second one, however, had had its guts ripped out, and inside had been installed a neat little radio set, with the terminals on top acting as the tuning and volume controls. The real joy of the thing, however, was the means of listening to it. A pair of headphones, if discovered, would speak for them-selves, and might be difficult to hide in a hurry in the event of a surprise search.

The batteries lived on the ground outside the hut: but the radio was linked to two highly-polished nails in the hut floor above them. In the hut was a small table, on the bottom of two legs of which were two equally polished nails. Placed in the right position, the table was 'electrified' – but just a quick nudge to one side and it was totally and immediately disconnected. One of the legs had been carefully hollowed out, and inside the hollow was the radio ear piece. A doctor's stethoscope, placed in just the right position against the hollowed-out leg gave perfect reception – and if the Nips came round on a surprise inspection, a stethoscope lying on an otherwise 'dead' table would be unlikely to arouse suspicions.

There remained the problem of how to keep the battery re-charged, which was where the introduction of mains electricity to the camp brought such relief to my unit. In that first house, on day one of our sojourn in Changi, we had found a gramophone. It was an old pre-war gramophone, which ran from a clockwork motor with a heavy spring, which had to be wound up by hand before playing each record. It suited our purpose admirably. The inside was removed and replaced with a small generator, which was driven by winding the handle. By winding strenuously for what seemed hours (we took it in shifts for ten minute stints) we could charge up our radio battery. It was the relief from this quite tiring chore which made us so pleased to welcome mains electricity coming in.

The news was disseminated very, very carefully. Every night, Sergeant Davies, my Senior Wireless NCO, who slept next to the table and ran the set, would listen to the BBC at midnight, to Melbourne Radio at 12.30 a.m., and to San Francisco at 1 a.m. I went along and listened for myself once or twice, which was sheer Heaven – but I couldn't go very often, as we tried to have as few people as possible know where the set was kept, and a regular midnight trek by me would soon have become too obvious. Davies, who was an absolutely first-class man, therefore used to come and see me every morning sometime before 10.30 a.m. and give me a summary: and then at 11 o'clock I attended the Camp Commander's daily conference and said my little piece. The conference was attended by all the other Unit or Regimental Commanders, and thus through them it went back eventually to everyone in camp, a strict rule being that it was only to be passed on to little groups of ten men at a time, to avoid the risk of some Nip seeing a whole lot of men listening attentively and looking happy. As a further precaution, if we had any particular good or exciting news, we would hold it back for several days, so that any undue jubilation would be delayed until the cause was no longer so apparent.

We were therefore quite well in touch with the way the war was going on outside. We knew how many ships were being sunk, how many aircraft were being shot down, and where any battles were being fought: though it rather depressed us as we gradually came to realize that all the battles were being fought (and as far as we could see were going to be fought for a long long time ahead) in Europe or North Africa, and that South-East Asia had virtually been written off until Hitler had been exterminated. But it was very much better than knowing nothing and being in the dark: in fact, as the Allies, according to the BBC, seemed to be doing pretty well nearly all the time, Hitler seemed to be quite unnecessarily obtuse in carrying on at all.

For the snippets of news of the type that the BBC didn't mention, such as the current price of whisky or haircuts, or whether American troops were really arriving in worthwhile numbers in England, or what the effects of clothes rationing were, we had to rely upon newcomers. Every now and then there would trickle in an airman who had been shot down, or some men picked up from a lifeboat. One of the most interesting parties was a whole crew of American merchant seamen who had been sunk and then picked up by a German surface raider. The Germans didn't go in for machine-gunning lifeboats, and so the whole crew was there: but they had to be handed over to the Nips (the Germans apologizing profusely for doing so) when the raider put in to Singapore for re-provisioning. The Americans' first impression of the Nips had not been favourable, and they left the Germans almost with regret. As they were being landed, a Nip had been beating up a British prisoner on the quayside, and without a word one of the Germans had walked across, picked the Nip up, and threw him bodily over the side of the dock into the water. He turned to the Englishman, clicked his heels and bowed, and then returned to his ship: German Navy, of course, not SS.

People like this were much in demand going round the camps and giving talks on how the world was faring outside of Changi; and we also had an influx of people from other and smaller camps in Java and the mainland of Malaya which were now being closed as the Nips concentrated everyone in Changi. Many of these had more disturbing stories to tell, for conditions in some of these smaller camps were far worse than anything which we ourselves had experienced. One quite large party of those taken prisoner up-country in the early days of the campaign had spent their first months of captivity in the old convict prison at Kuala Lumpur, terribly crowded and sparsely fed, and in close proximiy to their captors. They'd lost a hundred dead out of an original strength of around one thousand from either dysentery or beri-beri (a nasty disease caused solely by lack of vitamin B in the diet), and had had the additional unpleasantness of being housed next to the interrogation room, wherein the Kempi (the Nip Gestapo) were wont to 'question' native political prisoners. The Nips, of course, always treated other Asiatics far, far worse than they treated us: hot irons to the genitals, the 'water-trick' of putting a funnel into the victim's mouth then pouring in several quarts of water before jumping up and down on his stomach or belabouring it with a rifle-butt, the wet towel round the head trick (fed with boiling water), forcing a man to kneel on the sharp upper ridge of a triangular baulk of timber whilst he had to hold up a 4 gallon petrol tin (full, and thus weighing 80 pounds) above his head, were all used to vary the common dog whip or rattan. Regularly, for two hours a day, our men could hear the political prisoners being 'questioned' – they couldn't hear the questions and answers, of course, merely the screams of the gentlemen being questioned – but although many scores were tortured, few lived to tell the tale afterwards, for whether or not the victim gave his information, those who hadn't already succumbed to the treatment were usually beheaded.

Six British prisoners had actually tried to escape from Kuala Lumpur: but before they even reached the coast, where they had hoped to find a boat, they had been re-captured and brought back. They had been kept in one small room for ten days on a daily pint of water apiece, with no food and without so much as a bucket in lieu of toilet facilities: then they were brought out and, in front of all the other prisoners who had been paraded for the purpose, each one had been issued with a shovel before they were loaded up into a truck and driven off in the direction of the cemetery. Nothing more was heard of them, but the Nip in charge had explained to the parade that the shovels were for them to dig their own graves.

British prisoners were not, on the whole, beheaded – this was reserved for Asiatics. But the Nips were really quite fond of it as a practice, their officers particularly being extremely proud of their big sharp swords: in Singapore itself, early on, they'd really gone to town routing out 'subversive elements', and to the glory of Greater Nippon had set up little trios of tall poles with heads on them – one Chinaman, one Malay, and one Tamil – at a number of main street corners, just to make it clear to the populace in general that being unfriendly to the conquerors didn't pay.

I heard of only two specific occasions on which British prisoners were beheaded. One was on board ship on the way over from Java, where a man in the urgent extremities of dysentery had been unable to wait to get permission before crossing over the deck to go to the lavatory, and had promptly had his head chopped off by a Nip Sergeant for disobeying orders: but the other case was not just done on the spur of the moment – it was done deliberately and cold bloodedly by our dear friends of the Kempi in Java, at a small early camp, and was witnessed by an officer who shared a bed space with me when we were building an airfield later on. The Kempi had picked up two men who were outside their camp foraging for coconuts, and had brought them back to the camp, where they turned out all of the officers and sergeants 'to see what happens to escapees'. The first one had been made to kneel on the ground, and the Kempi Officer had lopped his lolly with one blow of his sword; but the other had been less fortunate, if more spectacular, in his dying. He was spread-eagled on a hurdle, and then three Nip soldiers with bayonets had each in turn taken three runs at him – and then the Officer had stepped forward and shot him.

3   Selarang Square

My unit was to spend fifteen months in Changi before we were moved up country, and three milestones stand out – pay, the Red Cross ship, and Selarang Square.

From the very earliest days, as soon as the inner camp wire went up, various intrepid souls climbed out under the inner wire, then under the main perimeter wire, and contacted some equally intrepid Chinamen who set up in business a mile or so south. Initially the trade had been simply in food and cigarettes for personal consumption, but it was soon apparent that cigarettes could be re-sold within the camp at a very high profit. Nobody begrudged the 'marketeers' big profits – they were running very big risks if they were caught – but quite soon the cash available in the camp was running out. We had what we had brought in with us, but it didn't last forever. And then the marketeers discovered that the Chinamen were less interested in paper money (inflation very soon took off) than they were in valuables: gold signet rings, or anything else made of gold, watches, fountain-pens, or whatever. The marketeers started selling things on commission for the rest of us in camp, again at very high rates of commission – but again it was they who ran the risks. Some of them became quite rich. A few were caught, but nobody was executed, as threatened. If they were lucky, they would merely get beaten up and returned to their camp. If they were unlucky, they might get a day and night or so on the 'Tennis Court'. This was an abandoned hard court adjoining the house near the entrance to the whole of Changi which now served as the Nips' guard-house. If you were 'put on the Tennis Court' it was the old Nip trick of making you kneel whilst holding aloft a full 4-gallon petrol tin: and there you stayed even if you passed out through the extreme chill of the night or the tropical overhead sun (without a hat) during the day. The probability was that had the mere sentry shot someone, it would have to be reported to an officer, whereas a simpler punishment gave the sentry himself the chance to appropriate the booty.

The marketeers waxed fat, but the general attitude was 'good luck to them'. There was nobody else from whom you could buy anything, but you didn't *have* to trade with them.

Then things changed, at least to a degree. The Nips announced that they were going to issue pay. This is normal POW procedure – the capturing power issues a proportion of each POW's 'home pay', and eventually recoups it from the vanquished power.

The Nips, however, were not very generous. The scale was fixed at one Straits dollar for a private soldier, ranging up to ten dollars for a General (this was before the higher-ranking officers had left on Japan Party B). The Straits dollar was just over eight to the pound pre-war, and was worth around two shillings and fourpence, so a private soldier was not exactly overpaid, particularly as this was per month and not per week. We in turn scaled it down. Everyone was given his basic one dollar, but the excess over that, for Officers and NCOs, was split in half – half to him, and half to a Central Messing Fund. This meant that the Central Fund had some quite worth-while money.

As a corrolary to the pay, the Nips had authorized a Chinaman to come up to the camp once a week with unrationed food supplies. These consisted largely of cooking-oil, coconuts, bananas, dried fish, and a sweet sticky substance called 'Gula Malacca'. The Chinaman didn't come into the inner camps, and we had to collect bulk supplies from a central dump: but we opened up a little internal canteen at which individuals could spend their dollars whilst the cook-houses got something with which to flavour the rice.

It was not until September that the Red Cross ship arrived. We called it the Red Cross ship because the supplies came in a ship – but it was by no means a whole shipload. When we counted it, it worked out at five tins of corned beef, four tins of stew, some biscuits, and a hundred cigarettes apiece, with some communal items such as jam, powdered milk, and cocoa on varying scales of one tin between so many men. We put the whole lot, other than the biscuits and the cigarettes, into the cook-houses: by careful ekeing out we made it last for nearly four months.

In addition to the food, there were some drugs for the hospital (which were the most precious items in the consignment), and crates of clothing. The clothing was good, but limited in quantity. There were several thousand pairs of boots, a lot of hats, and just a few hundred shirts and pairs of shorts. Nearly every man who had no boots at all was able to be fixed up (with priority going to those who were fit and thus on the trailer-hauling parties); but as the other items only worked out at one between thirty or forty men, lots were drawn for these.

We rashly assumed that this would be the forerunner of regular Red Cross supplies: but in fact 'the ship' was the only one which ever reached us – there were no more supplies during the whole of the three years of captivity which awaited us.

Another good thing happened. The Nips issued us with 'field postcards' to send home. These were the usual wartime cards with a number of items printed in, and two little boxes at the end of each line which you could tick for ' Yes' or 'No', 'I am well' and so on. We were then allowed to add twenty words of a message of our own. We only got two more of these over the next three years, and it almost led to a row between me and my wife when the war was over and I got home.

'You only wrote to me twice in nearly four years' she complained.

'Three times' I replied.

'I only got two' she said. A month after I got home, the third one was delivered.

Those were the good things – pay, and the Red Cross ship. Selarang Square was less good.

The bombshell came in the form of a great pile of printed certificates, printed in English, and we were told that every man in the camp was to sign one forthwith. The forms read:

'I hereby solemnly swear, on my honour, that I will not, under any circumstances whatsoever, attempt to escape'.

Now as far as Changi was concerned, admittedly, the mere thought of escaping was one harboured only by raving lunatics: but none of us could tell what the future might hold, where we might be sent to, or even what Allied landings might take place near us. And in any event, the giving of one's parole is forbidden under British Military Law. Our Senior British Officer (a Lieutenant-Colonel by now, since this happened after the departure of Japan Party B) politely explained our position to the Nips, and returned the whole batch of forms unsigned.

This annoyed the Nips. They sent the forms back and made it abundantly clear that they weren't *asking* us to sign – they were *telling* us.

Our Commander refused. He explained to the incredulous Nips that we weren't just playing – we'd refused to sign and we meant it. We might be prisoners, but we still had principles and we still had consciences and we'd no intention of abandoning them.

The Nips lost their temper. They slapped our Commander's face, beat up the interpreter, and said that the forms should be given out to every man so that each could decide for himself. Then, if anyone persisted in this unbelievable folly, individual measures could be taken to alter any rascal's mind, and his blood, quite literally, would be upon his own head.

Although up until this stage all the talking had been done between the Nips and our Commander, our Commander had held frequent conferences with his Unit Commanders, and they in turn had passed the news down to their troops; so everyone in the camps had known how things were progressing after each interview. The issuing of the forms made not the slightest difference – we all felt the same way about the Nip demand – and on the following morning the 20,000 forms (there were only

20,000 of us left in Changi after all the numerous working parties) went back, unwrapped from their paper packets to show that they had in fact been distributed, although still unsigned.

From a spiritless, resigned, dejected, and apparently-cowed rabble, the whole camp had suddenly sprung to life. The effect on our morale was terrific. For the first time that most of us could remember, we were standing up to our captors: we waited in a state of high excitement, almost of elation or of jubilation, to see what the answer of the Nips (God rot them) would be.

In twenty-four hours it came: by the next evening everyone in Changi, with the exception of the hospital, would concentrate on Selarang Barrack Square.

Now, Selarang Square had been the heart of the old pre-war barracks of the Gordon Highlanders, and was now the inner camp nearest the main road and the guard room. It consisted of the standard design of a big central asphalt parade ground, flanked on either side and at one end with the other ranks' sleeping quarters. There were seven of these buildings, all identical, each of three storeys and each designed to sleep eighty-eight men, giving a total accommodation figure of just over 600; the whole area, buildings included, measured exactly 200 yards by 150 yards. On this little spot, for our sins, we were now to crowd 17,000 men (3,000 were in the hospital), with their cooking-pots, sanitation, and everything necessary to keep themselves alive for how long we didn't know, but for that matter at the moment didn't care.

At dawn the following morning, whilst the cooks cooked a double-sized lunch to keep us going all day, reconnaisance parties went over to Selarang to split the area up and allot space to individual units; I went along to receive my allotment on behalf of Corps Signals. The 11th Division camp, from the huts in the rubber-trees, was the smallest in Changi, and now had only about 2,000 inmates: for these we were allotted one 88-man block – not too bad compared with, for instance, the Australians who had two blocks for over 5,000. However, 2,000 men in accommodation designed for only eighty-eight was, putting it mildly, going to be a bit overcrowded. When we'd chalked out our spaces, we went back to our men: that afternoon we loaded up our cooking-pots, rations, and a stock of firewood onto trailers, hitched ourselves happily to the ropes in front, and dragged them over to the Square.

As we got near the edge, we had to unload and hump the stuff, as the orders were quite clear that once you were on the Square you stayed on it, and space was far too precious to clutter it up with such bulky things as trailers. Right round the edge, beyond the buildings, ran a road; and on this, a special force of Nip sentries brought up from Singapore was patrolling with fixed bayonets and obviously enjoying themselves hugely. Anyone already 'on the Square' who put a foot over the drain and was thus 'off the Square' was promptly acquainted of his transgression by a thud between the shoulders with a rifle-butt or a slap across the face (also with a rifle-butt) depending upon which way he was looking. At the four corners of the Square the Nips were erecting sand-bagged machine-gun emplacements.

As soon as we were all in, the Nips summoned our Commander and told him of their intentions. Here they had put us and here we should stay until we had signed the certificates. It was therefore entirely up to us. Two stand-pipes would be left running, so we shouldn't be wholly without water; but they would provide us with nothing else whatsoever, and no one would leave the Square for any purpose whatsoever. Men who fell sick could not be sent out to the hospital (where what few drugs we had left, apart from those in Unit MO's kits, were kept); and if any man died we were simply to dig a hole and bury him. Above all, we should not be allowed out to fell or to bring in firewood. Now that may sound trivial, but in point of fact it was the most damaging veto of all, for although we had emptied the central supply dump and brought in enough rice for maybe three weeks, dry rice is useless unless you can cook it, and we had firewood for at the most three days.

It was, however, much as we had expected, but an unexpected twist, and an ugly one, was given to the situation by the Nips announcing that they held four hostages: men whom they'd caught outside the wire a day or so ago, and whom they now intended to shoot as 'escapees' unless we signed the certificates within twelve hours.

Now the Nips knew just as well as we did that numerous men went out through the wire each night on 'trading parties': but the accepted punishment in the rare event of detection had never been anything more than a beating-up and a day or so on the Tennis Court. And these four men who'd been picked up had been no more 'trying to escape' than they had been trying to have triplets. However, with broad smirks, the Nips observed that as we were all so adamant about refusing *not* to escape, these men, quite obviously, had been on their way home to England: and as a result the penalty which, from the earliest days, had always been threatened would be exacted. Furthermore, they would be publicly executed in the middle of the Square for all to see.

Cold-blooded murder in public was rather more than any of us had reckoned on: but although our Commander protested violently, he also pointed out that our decision to refuse to sign remained unaltered. And so the matter rested, with the hostages in the guard room, the Nip sentries on the ring road and manning the machine-gun posts, and the rest of us defiantly on the Square.

That first night was a disturbed one. We crowded into the buildings at 500 to a floor, but even so there wasn't enough room for everyone inside, and many of us overflowed into the open air around the edges of the parade ground. I say 'the edges', because the middle wasn't available.

Although all the buildings had been designed with proper lavatories, the only running water we had was from the two stand-pipes on the Square. The lavatories were thus all out of order: but 17,000 men have quite a large internal capacity between them, and something had got to be done to cater for it. The only answer was the parade ground. After all, we only had 200 by 150 yards to play with altogether, and a lot of it was covered by the buildings. So the centre of the parade ground it had to be, and the centre of the parade ground it was.

The limiting factors were the thickness of the asphalt and the fact that we only had a total of twelve picks in the camp. We had plenty of shovels, but the asphalt was hard and thick, with a good solid layer of hardcore underneath, and rocky earth below that. Relays were organized which had started digging even before we moved in, and they dug solidly all through the day and through the night, through every day and through every night, for our whole stay on the Square. Men with baskets formed other relays which carried the rock and rubble away to a great heap at one end, stumbling along in utter darkness for the first hours until the moon came up, as the Nips would allow us no lights of any kind, yet the urgency of the job allowed no respite.

Construction, for all the feverish haste, barely kept ahead of consumption. We dug the pits 12 feet deep by 30 feet long, but each was filled by the time that the next one was ready. There were no seats, just slats with gaps in between, on which one crouched, and there was no need for lids – a queue hundreds long made sure that every vacancy was taken up immediately. As soon as a trench was filled the slats were moved to the next trench, and the first one roughly covered in with rubble: to try to keep down the pace at which the trenches were being filled, it was made a punishable offence (enforced by watchful patrols of Military Police) to fail to distinguish between these main latrines and the separate urinals which had been dug elsewhere and which had a better chance of draining.

Our first night was anything but peaceful, for in addition to the noise of the diggers digging, the shifts were changed every twenty minutes to keep the picks in the hands of fresh and energetic men, and there was a general upheaval as men came and went from the sleeping areas to join the diggers and the basket carriers. At about 3 a.m. it started to rain, and all the men sleeping outside tried to cram in under cover: but my personal recollection, above all, was of a cockerel who couldn't get to sleep either.

This revolting bird was the treasured possession of a man who had captured it on a foraging party out through the wire one night, and was now fattening it up for consumption: although the bird had kept tolerably quiet early in the evening, when the moon came up it grew even more restive than the rest of us, and at midnight it gave up trying to sleep at all and started crowing at the top of its voice about once every minute.

Three or four hundred would-be sleepers, all within a dozen yards of the bird, were soon just as awake as it was, and lay there with murder in their hearts. Unfriendly mutterings gradually grew, until one warrior voiced everyone's feelings and shouted: 'Shut up, you long-necked bastard'. The cockerel either didn't hear or didn't care, and a few minutes later the same voice grated: 'Three more like that, and I'll wring your f...ing neck'. Unimpressed, the cockerel carried on, and the voice murmured: 'One'. A minute later he yodelled again, and this time several voices chorused: 'Two'. But with reckless bravado he gave a third rasping cackle – followed by complete silence.

Nothing at all happened, and we all felt a little let down by the apparent chicken-heartedness of the self-appointed hangman: but just as another frenzied solo started up in foolhardy triumph, the noise of a flurry of feathers announced the executioner, and the note changed first to an alarmed cackle and then to an agonized death-scream. It died beyond doubt without a solitary friend in the world; but even after its going, sleep came fitfully, and the night seemed interminable.

When at last the morning did come, I climbed up onto the roof of our block, from where one could see the whole panorama. Every balcony, every window, every inch of space everywhere was seething and swarming: men, water-trailers, ration-dumps, more men, cook-houses, dumps of firewood, men, more men, ducks and chickens and even a small herd of half a dozen goats belonging to one British Battalion – men in queues, men in little knots, small groups, big groups, sitting, running, walking, sleeping, sweating, swearing, digging, singing, queueing, chatting, carrying baskets of rubble. Up on the roofs men were fixing up little makeshift tents from their groundsheets to get some protection from the next downpour of rain, and at the side of the Square the doctors had rigged up a tent in which one man was to achieve the distinction of having his appendix out before we left there. And dominating the entire scene, the hectic activity of the trench-diggers in the middle of the Square, the long queues snaking away anxiously urging them to hurry, the growing heap of spoil at one end, and at the four corners the machine-gun towers, now complete with machine-guns.

To conserve firewood we immediately cut down to giving ourselves only two meals a day, and instead of each unit trying to run its own cook-house, we made unofficial pooling arrangements to get every scrap of heat out of every log. Apart from the cooks and the diggers, none of us had anything much to do: but by the time you had spent an hour in the water-queue to one of the stand pipes, another hour in the medical inspection queue, odd ten minutes here and there in the urinal queues and half an hour in the latrine queue, the day seemed to pass quite remarkably fast, and we were all agog discussing what was happening and what was likely to happen.

In spite of the squalor, in spite of the discomfort, in spite of the fact that we were already getting hungry, the spirit of the troops was colossal. After six long months of saluting and bowing to low-grade undersized coolies, of innumerable pinpricks, of face-slappings and of general degradation and humiliation, at last we'd made a stand and were having a trial of strength in which all of us were playing a part. So naive we were, and so little still did we know about Nip mentality, that we took it almost for granted that so long as we stuck to our guns and showed how serious we were in our refusal, even *they* couldn't *really* starve 17,000 men into submission over so trivial an issue. And for the whole of that first full day and through the second day, we cheered every announcement made (and they came out every few hours): our Commander had again seen the Nips, again refused to sign, and the Nips had again repeated their demands. The four threatened hostages still had not been executed, and we felt that time was on our side.

But as the second full day faded and the third night approached, a more far-sighted and perhaps wiser group were taking a somewhat different view. The doctors approached our Commander and expressed the opinion that neither starvation nor the Nip machine-guns presented anything like such a threat to our lives as did the menace of epidemic. With the huge concentration, the open latrines, and the improvised non-fly-proof cook-houses, they predicted that dysentery on an unprecedented scale would be sweeping through the Square within a matter of days, and that even if we stayed there for just one week and then returned to our areas, the damage would be done and it would have such a hold as to be beyond all possible hope of future control.

Furthermore, Changi had for some weeks already been suffering from a small outbreak of diphtheria, and whereas all the known patients had been sent off to the central hospital before the move to Selarang, numerous 'contacts' were here on the Square in our midst. Normally, 'contacts' were kept in their own inner camps, but in separate huts in isolation: now they were just loose with everyone else, as isolation on the Square was quite clearly impossible. Although the actual symptoms take some days to develop, some men almost certainly already had the disease and were spreading the infection around.

Thus, said the doctors, whether we eventually won our point over the certificates or not, if we stayed here much longer we were threatened with a probable epidemic of diphtheria (for which we had no serum) and also with an absolutely certain wave of dysentery which, in the monstrous proximity of the Square, would spread with a rapidity a hundred times greater than anything experienced in the old medieval plagues.

The Nips were told, and hearing this chuckled with glee. Hunger and disease were precisely the screws they had meant to apply by the enforced concentration; and now that it was working and we realized that it was working, they fairly chortled with unholy joy. When we asked if we could at least evacuate the diphtheria patients as they fell ill, they replied that we knew the conditions: not one man left the Square dead or alive until we had signed. However, by way of a concession, since they knew that our twelve picks were fully occupied on the latrines, they would give us two more with which to dig the graves of our diphtheria patients.

All through the third day it rained, and so most of us got soaked. Our Commander had several more interviews with the Nips, but all that he got each time was further insult and abuse. We'd used up virtually all of our stocks of firewood, all of the window-frames, all of the doors, and every scrap of wood about the buildings had been stripped out and the cookhouse fires were just, but only just, still going. Although the flies and blue-bottles swarmed around more thickly than I'd ever seen anywhere, so that even the dumbest of us were thinking as much about dysentery as had the doctors earlier, no one even talked about the possibility of giving in, and morale was if anything hardening. Men no longer sang, and we'd only had one meal since the previous day: but there was not one whisper of criticism of our Commander's attitude, and everyone was behind him to a man.

But then, once more, the Nips tightened the screw. Unless we climbed down and signed by that evening, the whole of the hospital would move over the next day and join us on the Square. No transport would be provided, not even trailers sent over by us with men to pull them: and so all 3,000 patients would either have to walk or would have to come on stretchers carried by their walking comrades or the hospital's doctors and orderlies.

In Changi, you had to be really quite sick to qualify for admittance to the already grossly-overcrowded hospital. The death rate was high, the drugs were running out or gone, and a fair number of the campaign battle casualties were short of arms or legs and we hadn't got any artificial limbs. To move the entire hospital on foot would have meant certain death for scores and possible death for hundreds more, but to our every objection the Nips made the same reply: 'Sign, and you can go back to your own inner camps, and the hospital will remain untouched. Persist, and your blood will be upon your own heads, and upon no one else's. People who refuse to obey orders cannot expect to be coddled'. And just to make it plain that their threats were not empty, they had decided after all to execute the four 'escapees' that evening, whether we signed or not. The middle of the parade ground was no longer fit to be graced by a Nipponese firing-squad; and so they would do it behind the guard room, and all Unit Commanders would be witnesses.

Sure enough, out our Unit Commanders had to go. The four men were murdered, and the hospital was ordered to stand by to move.

And that was enough. We signed.

Like 17,000 pricked balloons we saw our glorious high spirited gesture fizzle out and flop with nothing gained but a whole lot of new germs: at least it showed us unmistakably at last the true character of the Nips. The killing of the four men was in itself sufficient for that. There was no proper firing-squad, no blindfolds, no ceremony at all. Each man, battered, dishevelled, and bearing horrible testimony to the methods employed upon him and his colleagues during the last four days, to make them 'confess' and thereby give some semblance of legality to their slaughter, was simply told to chose for himself the actual spot where he would like to die, and one Nip soldier with a rifle took him off to do the job single-handed.

Details would be tedious. Suffice it to say that none of the Nip soldiers turned out to be a very good shot and not one of them managed to hole-out in one. One victim, indeed, as he lay squirming on the ground, had to be finished off by the Guard Commander with a revolver as the Nip soldier with the rifle had emptied his entire magazine into him, shot by shot, unsuccessfully.

So ended Selarang.

4 Counting the Vitamins

The months dragged by, from Michaelmas until Christmas then to Easter, and each day seemed remarkably similar to the last one.

By Easter it was well over a year since we had been captured, and above all else the effects of our diet were making themselves felt. From sheer lack of quantity we were generally weak and run down. In spite of nine or even ten hours' sleep a night we felt listless, we got abnormally tired from walking a couple of miles (let alone hauling a trailer for a mile), and we frequently had black-outs. But this was incidental – the real trouble was from deficiency diseases.

Just what 'vitamins' are I still don't know. If you've got them in your diet, you're all right – but if you haven't, you're deficient, and you get a deficiency disease.

There is a whole string of vitamins, lettered half-way through the alphabet: but the only ones that really worried us were vitamins A and B. Vitamin C is the one when, if you haven't got it, you get scurvy, as on the merchant ships of old – but somehow scurvy gave us a miss. Vitamin E held no terrors for us either: all that happens if you haven't got this one is that you go sterile – and how would a prisoner even know? But vitamins A and B are very bad things to lack indeed – if you're short of vitamin A you are apt to go blind: and by the end of the first year we had a whole block at the hospital blacked out and full of men who were blind or going blind from vitamin A deficiency.

Vitamin B is divided into a number of sub-groups: B1,

B2, B3, etc. – each controlling some specific disease, but each disease being quite unpleasant.

The first to affect us was merely a minor malady – minor to the doctors, but unpleasant enough for the victim. It was known as 'Changi Balls', in which the whole of the skin in your groin and on the scrotum rots away and leaves a raw weeping mass – painful, but nothing more than painful. A 4-ounce jar of Marmite (which is almost solid vitamin B) could clear up a case of Changi Balls within a fortnight: but although by some Heaven-sent inspiration the packers of the Red Cross ship had included quite a lot of Marmite, this was much too precious to be wasted on mere lack of skin around the crotch, and it was jealously guarded in the same category as drugs, exclusively at the hospital.

What Marmite *was* used for was the main vitamin B deficiency disease, beri-beri. Beri-beri takes a number of forms, the first signs usually consisting of a gross swelling of the feet and ankles, which at the same time go numb. Later, this turns to paralysis, or if you are unlucky the dropsy breaks out elsewhere: in the face, the stomach, or worst of all in the testicles. And it's *real* dropsy, not just a little bit of swelling: your testicles can go on swelling and swelling and swelling until they reach the size of coconuts when they burst and you die screaming in agony unless you were lucky enough to die first. It is not a pretty sight. Or the dropsy gets your heart – cardiac beri-beri – which is almost invariably fatal. Beri-beri is a very foul disease, and is quite unnecessary so long as you eat your vitamins. But our diet was short on vitamins.

Pellagra worried us a little bit, but not unduly. Nobody at this stage died of it, although a few went mad (it can do this), but most victims merely came out with frightful dark blotches all over, as it does something curious to the pigment of your skin. It was disfiguring, but nothing more unless it made your teeth fall out as it damages the gums. All this through lack of vitamin B again.

Therefore, vitamins to us were not just a 'food-fad' – they were really quite vital. And as most of the reports we got from in-coming parties from other larger camps (not the small ones) were of better and more varied food, we longed for the day when we too should leave Changi. Parties were still going away, and others coming in – Changi was the reservoir. And in April, the largest party to date was called for, 7,000 strong, to go overland as F Force.

There wasn't that number of fit men left in Changi: but the Nips said that that didn't matter – they were going up-country to far superior 'camps in the hills', so if anything the move would do semi-fit men good, and they'd have a better chance of recuperation. Eventually the Nips agreed that only thirty per cent of the 7,000 need be fit for normal duty, forty per cent to be classified as 'fit for light duty only', with the remaining thirty per cent unfit for any form of duty or even for marching.

They were all going from Singapore by train, and were told to take their baggage and cooking-pots and whatever else they liked. It was even suggested by the Nips that they should take a piano so that a concert party could be equipped at the other end. And so off F Force went, one trainload of six hundred a day for twelve days, in the highest of spirits and leaving Changi strangely empty and with barely sufficient men left to perform their own chores.

My unit was left.

We were left for two reasons. One, we were running the camp radio; and two, my particular unit, Corps Signals, although small, had the highest proportion of fit men in the 11th Division camp, and had been re-christened 'the administrative unit'. Fit men from other units had been drafted to me to keep me up to strength, and we did all of the wood-hauling and ration-drawing; we even ran an authorized garden in the outer area where we were growing vegetables to supplement our rations. This had got to be done by *someone*, and as my little unit was still small compared with the full infantry and gunner regiments, we were sufficiently marginal to keep out of the 7,000 without appreciably affecting it.

It didn't last.

Within a week of the departure of the last of F Force, a 'Borneo Party' was called for. Only 500 were required this time; but Changi was by now so thoroughly stripped of men fit for working, that I had to contribute one officer and fifty men.

I did so with regret. I had tried to keep my own officers and men together as a single unit: but I finally nominated Lieutenant Paul B———, and the fifty men. Paul was an extremely nice fellow – he was not one of my own original Corps Signals, but had been drafted onto me as a 'fit man'. He stood at around six-foot two, had stroked the Oxford boat shortly before the war, and had been contemplating entering the Church when war broke out and he had enlisted. I was sorry to see Paul go, but if anyone was capable of looking after fifty men, he was.

I have never forgotten one incident concerning him.

Amongst the supplies which we could get from the Chinaman after we had been given pay was 'rice polishings'. You have probably never encountered these, and my advice to you would be 'don't trouble'. They are disgusting.

Rice, in its natural state, comes with a husk and a white kernel: but between the husk and the kernel is a little brown 'inner skin'. Milling the husk and the inner skin off together is easy, and leaves the 'white rice' which looks pleasant and is what most people buy and eat. Taking just the husk off and leaving the inner skin leaves 'brown rice', but is a more delicate and thus more costly operation.

Needless to say, the Nips fed us on the cheaper white rice – but that inner skin contains vitamin B, which white rice does not. We needed vitamin B, to counteract beri-beri.

On the advice of my doctor (a young man who really knew his stuff), I bought the polishings. You couldn't get just the inner skins – you got the husks and skins mixed together. The Chinaman could get them, but they were not much in demand, and I got them very cheaply. But I was getting vitamin B.

There were only three effective ways of consuming them. You could eat a mouthful dry, but as it was ninety per cent husks, it was almost impossible. You could spread them over your meal, which made the whole meal virtually inedible. Or you could mix them up in half a mugful of water, and drink it hoping that it would not make you vomit: it frequently did.

I made myself unpopular (not for the first time). With

the impounding of Goldie's net I had ended up with the only cook-house and the only unit which hadn't got dysentery. I was determined to have the only unit which didn't get beri-beri. I made the consumption of rice polishings compulsory. At each midday meal I had two officers on duty at the cookhouse to ensure that each man took one spoonful of rice polishings (foul though they were) as he drew his ration – raw, over his meal, or drunk in half a mugful of water. The men didn't like it at first – but we didn't get a single case of beri-beri before we left Changi.

One day, Paul had been on duty with a certain Captain Y———, a regular officer who had also been seconded to me as a 'fit man'. Captain Y———, universally known as 'Yum-Yum', was a stickler for discipline.

He was allowing the meal-queue to go through at a fairly slow rate in that he insisted on seeing that every spoonful of polishings was duly consumed, and the queue was becoming restive. The men were hungry.

Then, one man vomited (a not unusual occurence). Yum-Yum kept the whole queue waiting while he waited for the man to recover and then ordered him to have another spoonful. It was at that point that Paul lost his patience, and made an unpardonable remark.

Yum-Yum appeared at my bedside, stamped his feet to attention, saluted, and said 'Sir. I have placed Lieutenant B——— under open arrest'.

'Yes' I said 'for what?'

'Insulting his superior officer, aggravated by the fact that he did it in front of our troops'.

'That sounds serious' I replied. 'If he is outside, wheel him in'.

Paul appeared, stood to attention, and saluted.

'I am told that you have insulted your superior officer in front of your troops' I observed. 'Is this true?'

'I am afraid that it is, Sir' said Paul. 'I could not help myself. I apologize'.

I turned to Yum-Yum. 'And what were the exact words?' I enquired.

He looked a little reluctant, and then said 'Perhaps Lieutenant B——— would like to tell you, Sir'.

'I'm not interested in what Lieutenant B—— might like' I replied. 'It is you who are making the complaint, and I wish to hear it from you. It is for him merely to agree or to rebut'.

Yum-Yum looked even more sheepish and replied 'He said "for Christ's sake stop acting like a little prick"'.

'Is that true?' I enquired of Paul.

'Yes, Sir,' he replied 'I'm sorry'.

'That was a highly improper remark to make to your superior officer' I told Paul. 'You are severely reprimanded. Case dismissed – but wait a moment'.

I turned to Yum-Yum. 'I have severely reprimanded Lieutenant B——' I said. 'But if I may proffer a word of advice to you, I would suggest that for Christ's sake you stop acting like a little prick'.

I don't think that he ever forgave me.

Paul (I have deliberately suppressed his surname) duly pursued his ambition to enter the Church after the war, and eventually became a Bishop.

5   A Long Journey

Only one week after the demand for the Borneo Party had come in, yet another up-country party was called for, this time for 3,000 men: to keep the rest of my little unit together I made no complaint, and we were drafted, intact, to form part of H Force, which was to follow F Force up-country.

We were glass-rodded. We did some careful packing – a heavy all-mains radio tastefully disguised as an unopened case of corned beef, and a very delicate little battery-operated set built in two halves into two standard water-bottles. These each had dummy tops which held a gill or so of water, so that even if they were picked up and examined they'd still look convincing and you could still get a drink out of them. And we took our 'gramophone generator' in case we could not charge up our batteries.

It was only later that we discovered that 'water-bottle radios' had been constructed by nearly every party, that we were by no means unique, and that the Nips were on to them.

H Force was 3,000 strong, and was due to move at one trainload of 600 men a day for five days. We were H.4, the fourth trainload, preceded by H.3 who were all Australians, and followed by H.5, who were all Dutch ex-Java. We had an even higher percentage of sick – sixty per cent – than had F Force: but we weren't unduly worried in that we too had been told to take a piano, and were looking forward with high hopes to this wonderful land, these camps in the hills, where even sick men would get their health back again.

On 8 May 1943, H.4 left Singapore.

The lorries arrived on time, and we went down, already sorted out into rail-truck loads of twenty-seven men to a truck. There would be twenty-two such trucks, making 594. Two further trucks more to take the Nip Guards and the six remaining prisoners, namely the six Senior British Officers who would therefore ride in state (if in low company) and would be there to pass on the Guards' orders to the men. Lastly, there would be a 'heavy baggage truck' for such things as our cooking-pots.

We arrived at Singapore station with two hours to spare, and so the Nips who had brought us down got us out and lined us up in the yard where we were all counted, truck by truck. We were then marched down to the platform, lined up opposite our trucks (the train was already waiting) and we were counted for a second time just to make sure. We were then told to get in, and we were handed over by the Changi Nips to the Train Guards, who were not Nips but Koreans.

The Train Guards let us be for half an hour, then had us all out on the platform again to count us for themselves. We got back in.

Each truck had either an officer or a Senior NCO in charge, who was called the 'Truck Commander'. Truck Commanders were called out and we all assembled at the entrance to the platform for the Korean Guard Commander to tell us what we were to do during the trip. Meanwhile, one of the other Korean Guards had been checking up for himself, and found that one truck only had twenty-six men in it instead of the prescribed twenty-seven. He raised the alarm, and every truck was turned out, and with terrific commotion the whole Guard, shouting excitedly, ran up and down counting every truck and raising hell. Each truck was one man short. It was nearly half an hour before the interpreter was able to sort things out and calm them down. The Truck Commanders were still at the end of the platform – one from each truck – at the Guard Commander's briefing-session, which accounted for everything.

The briefing-session proceeded, and it was very simple and to the point. The Guard, their Commander explained

(he himself was only a Lance-Corporal) was only twelve
strong, and so obviously couldn't personally keep an eye
on the whole train. Truck Commanders would therefore
be held responsible, and if any man escaped, his Truck
Commander would be shot for negligence in letting him
get away, whether or not he was subsequently recaptured.
Just like that. We were not to get out of our trucks unless
we were told to. When we stopped at stations for meals,
two men from each truck would get out, get the food in
buckets, and take it back for consumption on the
premises. That was all. He hadn't the first idea just how
long the trip would take.

We went back to our trucks and got in: then the Guard
turned us out for one final count, after which the train
started.

I was not the Senior British Officer on the train as my
150 Signals unit comprised only one quarter of the total.
Monty, a Major in the Royal Norfolks, had the largest
contingent and was senior to me anyway: so he was
number one. Pat Malins, an unattached officer, was also
senior to me, and was number two; whilst I, the 'Boy
Major', was number three.

Monty, with two of his own officers, shared the truck in
the middle of the train with the Korean Guard
Commander and half of the Guards, whilst Pat, my own
adjutant by the name of Forbes, and I were to share the
truck nearest the engine with the other half of the Guards.

The trucks were small all-steel box-cars, each with a
single central sliding door on either side, and one small
ventilator up near the roof at either end. They'd been built
for carrying rice, and so had not been designed with an
eye primarily for human comfort; and as Malaya's
railways were narrow gauge, the trucks were far smaller
than their UK counterparts – 15 feet long by a bare 6 feet
wide, which was not much for twenty-seven men. Each
man had rather less than 2 square feet, and there wasn't
even room for everyone to sit with his back against a wall:
half a dozen sorry outcasts had to crouch in turn on their
kits in the middle amidst the tangled mass of everyone
else's legs.

The train crawled along, stopping every two or three

hours for water, for fuel, and for passing south-bound traffic. It was a single-track line, and the passing loops were mostly located at wayside stations serving little villages. Whenever we came to a halt at one of these, hordes of native vendors immediately swooped upon us with baskets of pineapples, hard-boiled eggs, bananas, and papayas ('paw-paws' in the local lingo). The Koreans, so far from stopping us from 'having contact with or talking to' the natives, let us buy freely, and also bought food themselves. All the way up Malaya we treated ourselves to an orgy of fruit and boiled eggs such as we hadn't seen for a year.

Our half of the Guard wallowed heavily in paw-paws, and each time they cut one, handed slices round to us: whilst we in turn gave them peanut-toffee and bananas, and built up what we hoped would be a useful store of goodwill against the future.

They were quite well behaved little chaps on the whole. This was their first experience of dealing with prisoners; and as we'd clambered aboard at Singapore whilst they'd still been out on the platform, we'd grabbed the end of the truck nearest the engine, and thus left the future nuisance of sparks and smuts blowing in through the open door to them. Although there were only three of us against their six, we had spread ourselves and our belongings out as much as possible; and when they eventually got in we nodded condescendingly towards the other end of the truck and they took it like lambs. Pat Malins undoubtedly helped. Although whilst at Changi we'd had to take off our badges of rank we had now put them on again, and with his bright red face, bristling moustache, and a monocle, he looked every inch the former British Army Major: the Koreans were completely over-awed. Throughout the journey they kept docilely to their half of the truck, gave us no trouble at all, and seemed quite impressed to find themselves sharing a truck with two British Majors and a Captain.

We three, therefore, were really quite well off: but conditions in the crowded general trucks were nothing like so good. The trucks were virtually unsprung, and coupled with chains as goods-trucks usually are. They jolted and jarred with every slightest variation of speed as the chains first stretched to their limit and then the trucks closed up and crashed buffer to buffer. They clattered and clanked like an iron-founder's yard, making sleep and conversation equally impossible; and, crouched on their kits in their 2-foot squares, hemmed in by sweaty humanity, the troops were very soon yearning to get out and walk about and stretch.

At the wayside halts, the Guards let those off who needed to worship Nature: but as only the very largest stations had latrines, this was far from being an invariably salubrious process. All one could do was to hop over the hedge at the back of the platform – and as the whole of F Force and the first three train-loads of H Force had been hopping over those self-same hedges throughout the last three weeks, you had to be extremely careful as to just where to hop. We learnt our lesson at the very first halt – but we learnt the hard way.

The halts were not only very erratic, but also of varying duration. The engine would give just one little peep on its whistle and forthwith start moving. There were no guards waving flags or getting everybody aboard. Men would leap desperately back over the hedge and be hauled aboard the already moving train with their trousers in their hands: only those were allowed off who were driven by necessity, and it wasn't allowed just to get off merely to stretch one's legs.

Our first real chance to get out freely, relax and move about was at Kuala Lumpur, where our first meal was due. We'd been told before we left that we'd be fed there – but as we'd left Singapore at 3 a.m., after all the counting, we had foolishly assumed that this meant at lunch time. It was under 200 miles, and so nine or ten hours seemed reasonable enough even for the Nips: but we crept along so slowly, over so many temporary or badly-patched bridges, that it took over twenty-four hours and we arrived at 4 a.m. ravenously hungry.

We'd had a meal on the Saturday afternoon before we left Changi, and had brought with us three rice rissoles apiece for our Sunday morning breakfast. Thinking in terms of a midday meal at Kuala Lumpur, we'd wolfed these early, at around dawn; and so by now, at 4 a.m. on the Monday morning, we were famished, and our stomachs were rumbling like the empty and echoing caverns that they were. The eggs and the fruit bought from the natives *en route* had helped – but we'd seen no more vendors after dusk, and few of us had snatched much sleep during either of the two nights; so when at last we reached Kuala Lumpur we'd been thinking of little else but food and those long-vanished rissoles, and the prospect of a real meal filled our minds almost as much as the yearning to stretch our cramped and aching limbs.

The food was disappointing. Our instructions before leaving Changi had been that we must take with us two buckets per truck for the collection of rations; and although proper buckets had not been available, we had scraped together our quota in the ubiquitous 4-gallon petrol-tins and some cooking-pots. The drill, which we now put into operation for the first time, was that when we reached a station at which a meal was to be served, two men from each truck had to leap out with their buckets and form up on the platform, whence they were to be marched off to the cookhouse under one of the Korean Guards.

As they approached the Nip cookhouse a great cloud of flies would rise up into the air revealing two long rows of buckets already on the ground with the food in them cooked (some while ago) and waiting. One row held rice, and the other one 'stew'; one tipped a bucketful of each into one's own buckets and bore them off in doubtful triumph back to the trucks to appease the hungry multitudes. Although we'd got 4-gallon petrol tins ourselves, the Nips had only the standard 2½-gallon pails; and although the rice pails were usually full, the stew pails were never up to the top. Therefore, when it was split up amongst a truck-load of twenty-seven men, each got something under three-quarters of a pint of rice with half a pint of stew. The 'stew' was stew in name only, and not what one might have thought. It was merely lukewarm slightly greasy water on which floated some two dozen lumps of pork fat, each the size of a slightly shrivelled Oxo cube, surrounded by a sprinkling of what looked like grass but was actually chopped up onion tops. There were never quite enough bits of pork fat to give one to each man in each truck – but you did get three or four blades of onion tops, and the greasy water helped one to swallow one's portion of the cold, lumpy rice.

This first meal, which we got at Kuala Lumpur, and this unique interpretation of the description 'stew', was to prove the prototype of all but one of the other meals which we got on the journey. We had six meals altogether spread over five days and nights of constant travel, and our ravenous hunger by the end proved almost as great a bane as did the crowding and the wakefulness.

The station itself, at Kuala Lumpur, was a sorry sight indeed. Before the war it had been one of the show-pieces of the Far East: spotless, with a fine hotel and the whole built on an admixture of the architecture of a palace and a temple, and constantly busy handling a large volume of traffic. What it was now like outside, I preferred not to think – but we were not allowed outside anyway. Inside, it was filthy and neglected, and the Nips seemed to have no scavenging or cleaning system whatsoever. Piles of dirt, bits of fruit-skin, paper, muck, and rubbish of all sorts littered the tracks and the platforms alike. The cooking was being done in the middle of the main platform in a row of old oil-barrels supported on little mud and brick ramparts with open fires beneath, whilst up near the front of the train (where I was) there was a huge pile of logs to re-fuel the wood-burning engines, with a smaller pile of coal which they used to start the things up, which had been well trodden-around onto the platform. The paint was peeling from the walls of the buildings, and the whole place looked faded and shabby and forlorn and dirty, it not only looked it – it was.

We were not allowed off the platform, and so a long trench had been dug up through the tarmac to make a latrine, fifty yards or so beyond the cooking area. This did not contribute to the fragrance of the environment, but certainly helped to breed extra flies for the cook-house.

From one of the oil-barrel boilers we could get boiled water which was safe for drinking and also for making tea if we had any tea-leaves left from the rations brought from

Changi: some of us even got enough for a wash and a shave, and felt much better after. But most of the troops who'd spent the whole last twenty-four hours in the trucks were much too busy simply hobbling about, creaking in every limb, and trying to uncoil; and our stay, no matter how depressing to those who'd known the place in its heyday, was all too short, and we had to crowd back in.

Back we went to our trucks, and off we trundled as dawn was breaking. With the coming of daylight the native vendors appeared at each and every halt: but we'd very little money left, and most of us gave up fruit and stuck to eggs as being more nourishing if less filling.

At Ipoh we got our second meal, identical to the first. We also got a bath – or a number of us did – under the pump at the end of the platform from which the tanks of the engines were filled. Having thus set the precedent with our Korean Guards, we did this at most stations in future where it looked as though our halt might be for long enough: and we were getting so sticky and mucky that occasional showers were truly a godsend. Out the soldiery would leap from their trucks, stark naked and led by their officers, jostling the crowds of civilians of either sex out of the way as we raced along the platform to get under the pump: for although it was perhaps not particularly dignified it was very much safer to leave one's clothes in the truck rather than to take the risk of the train starting suddenly without warning and not being quite sure as to whose clothes were which.

At Prai, on the mainland opposite Penang, we stopped on the next night for our third meal, and we thought that things were improving. In addition to the rice and the customary stew, this time they gave us some fish: narrow little creatures, rather like thin sprats, 4 or 5 inches long including head and tail, dried and now very lightly fried, and as salt as the Dead Sea. We got one of them each, and welcomed them gladly, until our pleasure was somewhat marred by the announcement by the cook-house Nip that there were few facilities further north for feeding, and so this issue covered two meals in one – stew for one and fish for the other. However, there was only the one bucketful of rice per truck, with no question of re-fills: and so our two meals consequently consisted of two half-meals of the bulk rice with which to fill our bellies, but with separate meagre 'flavourings'.

On we went, till on the third afternoon we passed through Padang Besar, the last station in Malaya; and on the fourth morning we came to Haadyai, our first major halt in Thailand.

Haadyai was even dirtier than the stations in Malaya, the whole place being little more than one great straggling latrine. Troop-trains had evidently stopped there in the night, when there was no moon, there were no lights, and piles of filth lay about the yard and between the tracks: although we had a meal there and stayed for an hour, we were not allowed to leave the reeking siding on which our train had halted.

As soon as we had crossed the Thailand border, the Guards' attitude changed. They became much stricter about letting us off at halts, for any purpose whatsoever, and they kept us rigidly away from the natives. The buying of fruit and eggs abruptly ceased, and our hunger increased accordingly: although the few odd contacts which we did manage to make showed the ban to be without much meaning, as the Thais wouldn't even sniff at our Malayan money, and demanded payment in Thai ticals instead.

Prior to the Surrender the currency of Malaya had been the Straits dollar, the notes being printed in English, bearing the King's portrait, and worth just under half a crown a time. Very soon, the Nips had issued their own new currency – same size, same colour, still printed in English but saying 'The Japanese Government promises to pay ...': and instead of the King's portrait, each denomination had a picture of some local product. One denomination carried the picture of a banana-tree, and not surprisingly the whole lot became known as 'banana money'.

Banana money had lost its value very rapidly, inflation rocketing in a way never experienced in England. It was not too bad at this time, only fifteen months after the Surrender: but to give you some idea of its eventual magnitude, coconuts (a staple food in Malaya) cost eight dollars a thousand at the time of the invasion, or just under one cent each. By the end of the war they cost one hundred dollars *each*, if you were able to find one to buy.

Even at this time, on our trip up to Thailand, the Thais wouldn't touch Malayan banana dollars.

After Haadyai we continued to meander up the Isthmus, growing steadily more and more unhappy, many of the discomforts of the journey having a cumulative effect. From sheer exhaustion we kept falling asleep, but the bumping of the couplings soon woke us up again: and we got more and more tired, more and more hungry, more and more muscle-bound and more and more dirty. The overhead sun beat down fiercely by day and turned the steel trucks into ovens. The sides became too hot to touch, so one had to lean against a blanket: whilst the steel roof and floor batted the heat back and forth until the atmosphere almost solidified.

As we were no longer allowed to get off and get under the engine-pumps, the lack of washing facilities, in particular, began to tell. Crowded together in small dusty ovens, sweltering slowly through the tropics, a tangle of twenty-seven sweaty human beings can well out-rival a party of pole-cats: and the stench of hot, moist bodies in the general trucks was well-nigh over-powering.

Though too hot by day, we were too cold by night – for the nights were by now bitterly chilly; and our only effective ventilation being through the open doors, the choice lay between icy draughts or suffocation. Pat Malins, Forbes (my Adjutant) and I, sharing a truck with only six Korean Guards, were extremely lucky: but the general 27-man trucks were the very opposite of fun.

The dirty, smelly journey limped on, our hunger and the aching of our muscles and our weariness steadily growing worse; till at 7 o'clock on the Friday morning, after just over five days and nights of solid travel, we banged and clattered to a standstill and the Koreans started yelling at us to alight.

6 Bampong

We had had no warning (for instance, at the previous halt) that our journey was about to come to an end until the cries of 'all out' sent us diving into the corners of the trucks for our scattered bits of kit – for even a rice truck which has become one's temporary abode for nearly a week induced quite a measure of unpacking of one's belongings. We groped about in the semi-darkness praying that nothing should be overlooked, then scrambled onto the platform struggling grimly with buckles and straps and doing them up on the way.

We were told to unload the heavy baggage truck and to pile the contents in a heap at the edge of a loading-ramp; and then we filed out of the station in the gloomy greyness of the breaking dawn and fell in by truckloads strung out all along the village street in little blobs and waited whilst the Koreans made their usual enormous job of counting us. Being in the first truck, I was soon counted, and then made my way back to the truckloads of my Signals personnel. Knowing that the full counting would take twenty minutes to half an hour, I then left my men and wandered off in search of local gossip. I thought that for a start I would see what Monty Smyth, our H.4 Party Commander was getting up to with our hosts, and found him in agitated converse with a new one, an evil-looking Nip officer whom we hadn't previously encountered. Monty's agitation was understandable, for the Nip, who seemed to be a local staff officer of some variety, was just at that moment light-heartedly delivering some news which would have agitated a corpse.

With an ill-concealed smile he was telling Monty that although our eventual camp was still between 80 and 90 miles further on, there was no transport of any sort available for the rest of the trip, and that therefore we should simply have to walk. It might, he added casually, be possible later on to get a lorry for the heavy stuff like our cooking-equipment and our boilers: but even that was doubtful, since although there was a metalled road for the first 30 miles, after that it was merely a jungle-track which could only take lorries in favourable weather – and the monsoon was imminent. We would spend the rest of the day and the night in a transit-camp 'to give us time to recover from the train trip, which probably had tired us'; the next day we should be setting out on the first stage of our march. This present village we were in, a place called Bampong, had a transit-camp but nothing more, with no staff, no doctors, no hospital facilities or anything else: so, everyone down to and even including stretcher-cases would have to march or be carried on their stretchers, as there was no one here to leave them with or look after them if we left them.

Monty explained that there must be some mistake. We were H.4, a party with sixty per cent sick men, few of whom could march for 9 miles, let alone 90: diphtheria convalescents, first stage beri-beris, Pellagra suspects, men recovering from dysentery, a party that the Nips at Changi had deliberately encouraged us to make up in this way, as 'we were going to some fine new camps up in the hills, where sick men would have so much better a chance of recuperating'. Wasn't the Nip confusing us with some other, fit, working party?

No, said the Nip, he wasn't. He knew precisely who we were: H.4. Three days ago H.1, he grinned, had made just the same point. So had H.2. So had H.3. And so, for that matter, had F Force, train-load by train-load throughout the previous fortnight. Each and every one had said that the march, with their sick, would be impossible. And each and every one – and he grinned more broadly than ever – had made precisely the same mistake. It was not only possible – it was actually being done, now, at this very moment, by all the parties in front of us. We not only *could* march – we *would* march, all of us: 15 to 20 miles a day, or rather, a night. We'd march by night when it was cooler, and we'd rest by day. And we'd got to be clear of the transit-camp by the following evening as a further train-load, following us up from Singapore, would want it for *their* night's rest.

We protested. We argued. We pointed out that although we had left Changi relatively free from dysentery, we'd undoubtedly collected plenty of new cases from the filthy railway cook-houses on the journey and indeed had several men showing symptoms already. To march them would wreck them – they ought to be in hospital, and to march them for 90 miles carrying their kit would be little short of murder.

The Nip smirked.

Forty of our party, we pointed out, had actually been in hospital at Changi until the day before we left, and had been let out especially to come up to the 'better climate' to recuperate.

The smirk widened.

Thirty per cent of our entire party – nearly 200 of them – we emphasized, were medical grade C, unfit for any duties, let alone for a jungle trek.

He leered.

Whilst talking of trekking, we drew his attention to the fact that quite a lot of our men had no boots – they'd literally dropped to pieces during the past fifteen months, and we'd had no proper repair materials. And for the rest, such boots as did remain were certainly in no state to go tramping through the jungle in for miles and miles.

He laughed.

We argued. We reasoned. We got angry. We demanded to see the Senior Nip Officer in the area, which made him laugh even more. He *was* the Senior Nip Officer he told us, but the more we protested the more his delight in watching us squirm obviously grew, until at last with an airy wave of his hand he turned on his heel, remarking as he did so that if we had anything which we wouldn't be able to carry for the whole 90 miles we might just as well throw it away immediately, as otherwise it was simply a waste of energy carrying it even as far as the transit-camp.

Our personal belongings were still relatively few. We'd brought in little enough to Changi originally, but although short of clothes we'd accumulated all sorts of bits and pieces since the capitulation by buying, bartering, or finding them in the abandoned houses at Changi when we got there. Taking my own case as fairly typical, I had a Li-lo (punctured, but capable of being stuffed with straw to make a bed, or for use un-stuffed during the daytime as a waterproof cape), a battered enamel basin (liberated from a shattered gun-emplacement in the early days at Changi before we were wired in), a full-sized bath-towel (my pride and joy, which I'd bought off a Chinaman whilst I still had some money), a pair of heavy home-made wooden sandals, a hurricane lamp (from the self-same gun-emplacement), and a small home-made wooden stool, to mention the bulkier items only. We'd still got all of our Japan Party A 'warm clothing' which had never been recalled, and we all had such essentials as a plate, a spoon, a mug, a blanket, and unless you were unlucky a mosquito-net. Every man in the party carried one book from the library at Changi with which to start a new library at our new camp. Everything was old and worn and shabby and of virtually no intrinsic worth, but infinitely precious to men who had nothing else in the world and little hope of getting anything more until the war was over: that's why every man was draped-around like a Christmas tree. But when it came to sheer bulk, it was not so much these personal possessions which were staring Monty and me in the face like a spectre, as the unit heavy baggage – the communal equipment on which not just our comfort but our very future existence might depend.

You can't cook rice for 600 men in a 2-pint saucepan. We had several large coppers each holding 20 or more gallons, steel barrels (old oil-drums) for boiling water, and more oil-drums adapted as ovens. We had axes and saws for chopping up firewood, a grind-stone for making rice flour, and two precious panniers which held what had been our share of the drugs and medical supplies at Changi hospital and surgical instruments for our doctors. There were fifty trestle tables as the nucleus of our new camp's furniture, and a lot of benches to go with them.

In no way could we carry that lot for 90 miles, and so we perforce left the coppers, the oil drums and the tables and chairs on the loading-bay in the pious hope that the Nips would indeed send these on by lorry. Monty then called an immediate conference of Truck Commanders, who were each told to go back with one man to the loading-bay and collect the lighter things such as the axes and saws, the cook-house ladles and other equipment, the two medical panniers and the six stretchers accompanying them, and to divide them up on a 'one-item-per-truck' basis for us to carry to the transit-camp.

The Korean Guards stayed with the train, and we were taken over by new Guards – Nips this time. After a final truck-by-truck count by the new Guards, off we shuffled along what appeared to be the village's only street, until after about half a mile we turned off along a dusty track for another half mile or so and came to a group of filthy hovels already half-packed with prisoners.

Four long attap huts (the familiar dried palm-frond thatch) stood side-by-side end-on the roadway. Each consisted simply of a long central ridge-pole, supported at intervals by single uprights, with a roof sloping away on either side right down to the ground, like a couple of giant playing-cards resting together along the top edge. No matting or floor-boards or anything else covered the bare earth floors inside; and the open ends served the dual function of door and window, whilst half-way down (the huts were each a hundred yards long) rough flaps cut in the roof provided the only additional light and made one hope that it didn't rain.

Two of the four were already full of Australians, whom we found to be the party that had travelled up from Changi the day before us: H.3. Crowding round they told us that H.2, the party in front of them, had similarly been in residence when they'd arrived yesterday, and had marched out from the two huts now freed for us at 8 o'clock last night. That was the standard programme for the camp, parties getting in for breakfast and leaving after thirty-six hours, marching by night.

Full of foreboding we crowded into our huts, but although they were each about 20 feet wide and 100 yards long, this was nothing like long enough, and space was at a premium. Truck-loads kept together, and each was allocated 20 feet by 20 feet ('just enough room for a coffin apiece' as someone aptly put it): having moved our kit in, we rapidly moved ourselves out again into the semi-fresh air where the smell was less overpowering.

The huts stood back about 20 yards from the roadway with a narrow strip of ground between each hut and the two outer ones flanked by an extremely flimsy and somewhat intermittent bamboo fence. The back of the camp didn't end anywhere in particular, there being no fence but the shrubs getting taller and denser until one lost interest: this ill-defined compound, besides the four huts, boasted as its only embellishments a well, an enormous latrine, and surprisingly enough a Buddhist temple.

The temple, of course, had been there long before the camp, the Nips having chosen the site to get the use of the well without having to prospect for and dig one for themselves: it still remained in full operation with the bright-robed priests in their saffron habits strolling straight through our huts on their way in and out and to and from the road.

Inside, the huts were quite reasonably clean, but the rest of the compound was in an appalling state of dirt and neglect. The dismal, squalid little forecourt was simply a stretch of uneven, bare earth, with a wide ditch separating it from the road and overflowing with stinking refuse from end to end. Half-dried-up puddles were dotted about the area, choked with mucky litter; and accumulations of rubbish of every sort were scattered about, caught in the undergrowth, trodden in the mud, or heaped in mountainous drifts in odd corners.

A notice in English, headed 'Regulations for Coolies and Prisoners-of-War' was posted up on a large notice-board at the entrance to the camp. Although headed in the plural it stipulated only one single regulation, which ordered us to use the proper latrine instead of the surrouding bushes. The coolies who had preceded H Force obviously couldn't read, and evidences of their illiteracy were plastered in copious profusion about the shrubberies and even in the

drain trenches round the outside edges of the huts; flies in
their hundreds of thousands were eagerly feeding and
breeding and storing up even more dysentery for us.

The cook-house, on the other side of the road, was even
worse. We were not expected to cook for ourselves, and
this was a static cook-house manned by a mixed all-Asian
staff. A Nip soldier in charge, Thai women, Tamil Indians,
and the ubiquitous Chinamen all seemed to have their
grimy fingers in the pie; and, not being bound by the
'Regulations for Coolies and Prisoners-of-War', they
simply used the hedge behind the boilers for all purposes.

Seeing the food prepared, and the uninhibited habits of
those preparing it, would have completely quelled any
appetites less vigorous than ours: but after the last week's
semi-starvation, food of any sort seemed wholly desirable,
and most of us lapped it up without a thought as to the
probable built-in dire results.

They gave us our breakfast meal within an hour of our
arrival at the camp – a goodly dollop of rice with a fine
thick stew of yams and pumpkins, which we despatched
with great satisfaction, flopping down on the floor of our
huts and going to sleep immediately afterwards, revelling
in this, our first real meal and our first real rest since
leaving Singapore: and speaking for myself I slept like a
babe until we awoke at noon five hours later for another
similar meal – stew with more solids in it than just greasy
water!

Wolfing a further pint of rice and this wonderful stew
we felt a good deal happier, and began to look around for
somewhere to clean ourselves up and to wash our
excessively travel-stained persons. Standing up like an
island in a sea of trampled and swampy mud, the well was
ringed around with scores of grimy prisoners: the solitary
bucket which the well could take at a time being in
constant use, the best we could do was to tip it rapidly
over each other and then retreat to carry out more detailed
operations in a little saved in a mug or in a mess tin.

Feeling refreshed, if only marginally less grubby, we
next found our attentions completely taken up with the
natives. Gathering in the roadway and on our puddle-
bespattered forecourt, dozens of Thais were rapidly

forming a little impromptu bazaar. Most of them carried wide flat baskets full of bananas or mangoes; some had hard-boiled eggs, peanut toffee, or gritty sago cakes, whilst still others had little charcoal fires in battered biscuit tins on which they were frying omelettes, cooking mah-mee, or boiling coffee.

After a year of one extremely limited canteen, we felt like a bunch of Eskimos given the run of their teeth in the Savoy Grill; but although at first we were almost overwhelmed by the profusion, we soon discovered the snag to be our almost total lack of Thai money. The Nips had refused to change our Malayan banana money into ticals: the vendors, not unnaturally, demanded local currency, and the odd few who were willing to take Malayan dollars did so at a substantial discount, demanding up to twenty dollars for one tical.

The difficulty, however, was rapidly finding its own at least temporary solution. Fortunately, we had ignored the Nip officer's suggestion down at the station that we throw away everything which we couldn't carry for 90 miles there and then, and we had staggered with it up to the transit-camp. Now, we found a ready and eager market ready to snap it up, for cash.

Nip troops, in two's and three's, came sneaking into the huts, intent on buying up all they could of our treasures at knock-down prices. With big expansive smiles they'd approach a group of prisoners, totter about in realistic pantomime aping a man with a huge imaginary burden staggering and dropping to his knees and then rummage about in our kits and pick out likely objects, tantalizingly waving a handful of tical notes in our faces. Even a Nip officer (not our friend from the station) came in trying to buy a Sam Browne belt – but he was unlucky, no one having one left for sale: but although in their efforts to corner the market for themselves they issued strict orders forbidding us to trade with the Thais and chased off all competitors, they were very soon completely overshadowed by the natives. Whilst the women and children were hawking their fruit and eggs on the roadway outside the forecourt, half the male population of the village came swarming around the back near the temple, brandishing

whole bundles of ticals and scrambling for anything and
everything we offered.

Most of our saleable 'surplus property' took the shape of
spare bedding or clothing, and many of those who had an
extra blanket, more than one shirt, or a spare pair of
shorts, weeded them out and flogged them whilst the
flogging was still good, rather than running the risk of
finding their load too great later on in the march. Shirts
and pairs of shorts, no matter how tatty and worn, were
passing freely at up to five ticals each, whilst hitherto-
unused Japan Party A heavy clothing went like wildfire.
Everything found a ready market, and so produced a few
invaluable ticals.

Best of all were the prices being obtained for trinkets
and valuables. Anything made of gold or silver got the
buyers running and had them bidding against each other
in a sort of unorganized auction: rings, cigarette-cases,
cigarette lighters, and topping the bill as the biggest
attraction were fountain pens and wrist watches. Value,
more often than not, depended largely upon flashiness,
with the curious twin exceptions of Parker pens and Rolex
watches. These, apparently the only names to penetrate
darkest Asia, fetched as much as treble the highest prices
paid for other makes, irrespective of how well-known or
expensive the others might be at home – a striking tribute
to the power of modern Anglo-American advertising.

By tea time, trading had reached a fever-pitch of
activity. Everywhere one looked one saw men slinking off
into the bushes at the back, pairs of trousers or rolled up
mosquito nets tucked under their arms: whilst in those
bushes and welling through all the numerous gaps in the
fences, scores of clamorous Thais were making the most of
a lifetime's opportunity.

Every now and then a patrolling Nip sentry would
cause a momentary panic, chasing the natives and beating
up prisoners who hadn't got away in the general
confusion; but although a number of men got hefty clouts
on the heads or kicks on the shins, nothing serious
happened, and it had no effect whatsoever on the
continuing trading.

Even crossing the road to the cook-house one would find

oneself accosted by a native tugging urgently at the sleeve of the shirt which one was wearing, muttering 'Mister! T'ree tical': I myself was involved in a highly undignified chase and a squabble, my plate being snatched from me by an eager young Thai woman who simultaneously thrust a fifty-cent note into my other hand before running off. Fortunately she slipped in the mud and fell down, and I was able to catch up with her: whereupon a helpful bystander, seeing me waving the fifty-cent note in my hand, called out 'Fifty cent no good. Nice girl. One tical' – evidently mistaking me for a would-be client for personal services, for which I was offering below the going rate.

Thais and prisoners alike regarded each other with the utmost suspicion – they, refusing to part with their money until they had handled the goods; and we learning only too rapidly their tendency to run away without paying at all. A curious sort of snatch-as-snatch-can was in vogue as a consequence, whereby the two parties danced about, feinting and crouching like a couple of all-in wrestlers seeking an opening, with us attempting to grab their money before we gave them the goods, and them intent on seizing the goods and darting away through the crowd without paying.

A system less liable to deadlock soon evolved, more formal but quite as picturesque. We and the Thais placed the goods and the money on the ground at a distance of about 3 yards apart: the Thais counted out the notes for us to see, and then, at a given moment, we each dived towards the other's pile. This did away with the former danger of where the Thais did in fact hand over some money, but usually in a little roll which, by the time that we ourselves had counted it, was frequently found to be somewhat short of the price which had been agreed.

A regrettable number of the Thais were there primarily for a little thieving rather than for honest trade, and most of the others would filch if they got the remotest opportunity. Several unfortunate fellows were robbed of their boots whilst bathing naked at the well, whilst one had his trousers stolen before his very eyes whilst crouching over the latrine. He'd taken them off and hung them on a bush just out of his reach; and the brazen Thai who did the deed took a most unfair advantage of the difficulty of immediate and modest pursuit to jeer at his victim and to make a rude noise at him prior to running off, leaving the erstwhile owner to creep back trouserless to the hut.

Much as I wanted some money, I clung to the little bit of possessions which I had, still harbouring dimming hopes that transport arrangements might yet be made; but David Eastham, one of my Signals Subalterns, sold his watch for the excellent figure of eighty ticals, and most generously gave five ticals apiece to each of other Signals Officers which, in the bazaar, would go far on food.

I, as did most of the others, invested fifty cents in a hot freshly-cooked mah-mee – a fried concoction of little bits of chicken meat, chopped up vegetables, beansprouts, onions, chillies and sauces, with a couple of eggs broken over the top, all knitted together and woven around with spaghetti-like mee (a local noodle); fifteen cents bought a pint of surprisingly good coffee; and then got going on the mangoes. These, we were sneeringly told by those who claimed to be mango connoisseurs, were wretched little specimens, only about 4 or 5 inches in length: but we of the untrained palates found them deliciously sweet and juicy, and the vendors had all we could buy at four for ten cents. I ate a dozen without serious difficulty, although I had to pay a visit to the well to remove the surplus juice from my elbows: and then I returned to the hut to lay out my kit for the Nips' inspection.

As was usual with Nip inspections, we'd had plenty of previous warning, the Australians having told us as soon as we arrived to expect a search in the evening. Our hosts up here, they said, seemed to be suffering from radio-mania, and were confiscating everything remotely electrical, as well as tools of every description: but as each party had duly been warned by the party before them what to expect, results, except from the very first train load, had been somewhat disappointing.

What made it so ridiculous was that there was no segregation of the two Australian huts from ours, but the Nips only 'searched' the new arrivals. As the Australians had been searched the day before, it would be perfectly safe for us to hand over any contraband, such as radio sets which we might have, to them until our search was over, and they could then give it back to us. It may sound silly, but that really *was* the way in which the Nips operated, and we had duly lodged our contraband with the Australians before 5 o'clock, when the search started.

The farce over – it lasted for nearly an hour – they left us in comparative peace. Until it grew dark we spent the time eating mangoes and smoking a Thai cigarette called 'Red Bull' which was available in the bazaar and although repellent enough was the nearest to smokeable tobacco we had met in over a year, and streets ahead of the Chinese-Malayan excrescencies we'd occasionally managed to get in Singapore.

At dusk the Australian party fell in, and after much bother and shouting and counting by the Nips, they moved off on their way: seeing this for ourselves, the Nip officer's boast that we not only *could* but *would*, seemed to underline the futility of hoping for any improvement in the outlook.

Twelve hours' sleep did much to revive our spirits as well as our bodies, although the prospect could still justify little boisterous optimism. During the morning, the British Commander of the whole of H Force visited the camp with the latest news; but although he produced a single ray of watery sunshine, everything else he had to tell us was as gloomy as it could be.

He himself had come up on the first train five days earlier and had gone on up to the second and third staging posts and then returned: but although he'd been plugging away at every Nip he met, so far he'd had no success whatsoever in getting things put right. Every party to date had had exactly the same reception as we had; all had voiced exactly similar protests and been similarly ignored; and all, in spite of tactics ranging from violent objection to grovelling plea, had had to march out complete with their sick and their minimum portable baggage as ordered.

When he had first arrived, the Nips had silkily spoken of 'staging-camps', saying that parties would march a distance of only 25 kilometers a night, and would spend the intervening days at these camps where they'd rest and receive meals cooked for them by Asian staff from semi-permanent cook-houses. That was before he had gone up to see them for himself; but now that he had seen the first two camps on the route, he had found out enough to make him thoroughly depressing company.

The first camp consisted simply of a native school, built in the local style raised on piles with a space underneath. The Nips themselves were using the school, and all that the prisoners got was the space on the bare ground underneath. There was room for at the most 200 under this cover, the other 400 men simply sleeping in the open round about. There were few native vendors compared with Bampong, and no local staff for the cook-house, which we would have to run ourselves.

The second was even worse. The only building was used as the cook-house, and round about it was nothing more than a patch of fenced-off scrubland, with no protection from the elements. Water had to be bought from a neighbouring village at five cents a bucket, and although the Nips had now been persuaded to commandeer enough for cooking, all above that, for drinking and washing, had to be bought by the prisoners at their own expense.

No arrangements of any sort had been made for the sick at either camp, and herein lay the real heart of our problems. Men who were reasonably fit were coming to little harm, apart from blisters – for decrepit boots with no socks meant plenty of blisters which burst and turned septic – but scores of the sick, who were far too ill to move even by Nip standards, were finding the strain too much, and were breaking down in their droves at every halt.

A march of 16 miles with their baggage, night after night, is no fit programme for men who are bleeding from the bowel with dysentery, shivering with malaria, or swollen and numb with beri-beri: and yet our captors, completely indifferent to how much suffering they caused or how many men died, were forcing these helpless victims to carry on stage after stage until they finally collapsed.

Every evening, before the parties marched out, the Nips themselves conducted a comb-out of those too sick to go and decided who should continue. The basis on which they worked was not of whether a man was sufficiently strong to get through the whole of the next night's march, but solely of whether or not they could get him onto his feet and make him start: and if they could, and he covered the first half mile, they drove him relentlessly on, until he collapsed by the roadside and couldn't be revived either by rifle-butt or boot, or reached the next camp utterly broken, there to join the abandoned dregs of the cripples from previous parties.

Efforts to get things done were completely hamstrung by the impossibility of contacting any Nips in positions of real authority. We, of course, could not leave our camps to seek them out (and wouldn't have known where to look for them) and so could only wait and see such Nips as chose to come to us: and as all of those in real authority took good care to keep well away from us, we found our approaches confined to our private-soldier guards or odd NCOs of their administration. The guards were merely blindly and mechanically carrying out their orders being themselves very much second-raters rather than 'fighting men', genuinely incapable of independent thought and knowing only that they would be flogged if they failed to obey.

It was they, by the threat and the free use of force, who were pushing the schedule through: and in spite of all the complaints they were plodding forward with terrible single-mindedness, every party so far marching out on time, driven on like cattle. Fit and sick alike were being herded along the trail till they dropped, the guards in the rear keeping stragglers going with rifle-butt or boot: and those who did drop were very soon goaded back into the column, or if they had fainted and didn't respond to the usual kicks in the stomach or groin, were left as they were by the roadside to die or fend for themselves.

As a mental urge the Nips kept saying that once we got to the other end, we'd find that everything would be all right: but our Commander observed that after seeing the blots they so glibly referred to as 'staging-camps', he, for one, had lost all faith he had ever had in their promises. And we, although we'd been assured at Changi that we were bound for fully-equipped, fully-prepared camps, we too were now beginning to doubt whether even these were quite so fine as they sounded.

One thing, however, was perfectly clear, and that was that we must get as many of our men through as possible. These would at least have our MOs and orderlies to tend them, whereas those left *en route* would simply have to take their chance. The Nips refused to let any fit men stay behind at any of the staging-camps to look after them, so that they had to rely for cooking, wood-chopping, and water-drawing on subsequent parties coming through: although at the second camp, Kamburi, there was at the moment an F Force MO, himself sick, in charge, as soon as (or if) he got well, he'd be obliged to march on like anyone else.

Our Commander confirmed that F Force, the 7,000 party who'd left Changi before us, had passed along this same unhappy route; but they were bound for camps as far away as 190 miles against our mere 90: remnants of their very sick were scattered along the dreary trail, reports suggesting that camps beyond Kamburi (where the metalled road ended) grew steadily worse.

The only cheerful note which the Commander was able to sound was in connection with baggage. On this, he had managed to extract a promise from the Nips to send it on as soon as possible, and not only the unit heavy equipment, but 'private' packs and bed-rolls as well, as long as we clearly marked them. A truck would come up from the station this afternoon and collect these and take them down to the dump: and the Nip had promised faithfully to send it all on within three weeks at the very latest.

Feeling extremely glad that I hadn't started selling kit yesterday, I went away to re-pack my belongings in the light of this new development. I reckoned that, being fit, marching 90 miles would pose me personally no problems; but the more that I tried to carry on my back, the less my chances would be. I therefore resolved to limit myself to the very bare minimum needed for three weeks, and to stake my all on the Nips fulfilling their promise to send the rest on.

All that I proposed to take was a couple of light haversacks rather than a heavy pack, slung separately from shoulder-straps. One held a blanket, a pair of socks (I was lucky enough to have a spare pair) and a shirt. The other (a very small canvas affair) held my mug, plate, and spoon, and some washing things. Under the flap I was able to stuff my Li-lo to serve in the now triple capacity of groundsheet, bed, and waterproof cape; and everything else I steeled myself to leave with the heavy baggage, for although there was a fair number of items, each of them weighing very little, the slightest addition would have meant a pack instead of a haversack. Although it tore my heart to part even temporarily with my wash basin, a pot of Marmite bought on the Black Market, my Japan Party A clothing, and sundry minor items, all were carefully wrapped in my proper groundsheet with my mosquito-net, my second pair of shorts, my shoes, and my heavy towel.

Having thus, albeit with some trepidation, shot my bolt, I placed my roll on the pile by the entrance, had another delicious mah-mee, loaded some hard-boiled eggs for the trip, and spent the rest of the afternoon asleep to gather strength for the night to come.

7 On the Way Again

We had a final meal from the cook-house at 5 o'clock and then at 6 o'clock we formed up on the roadway. We were still kept in 'railway truck-loads', and we were kept there being counted for a good half hour, after which we waited for another full hour whilst it grew dark: at half past seven the Nip officer whom we'd first met at the station yesterday morning arrived and summoned a meeting of all Truck Commanders.

He gave us our instructions for the march, which were simple. The three Senior British Officers, which meant Monty, Pat Malins, and me, would be at the head of the column with two Nip guards. Truck-loads would stay together and at the rear would be our two MOs with two more Nip guards. We were going to march by night 'by easy stages', and the head of the column would set a gentle pace with frequent halts, and therefore there would be no excuse for anyone lagging behind and Truck Commanders would be responsible for seeing that all their men kept up.

By way of emphasizing how undesirable it was for men to fall out, he mentioned casually that the natives we might encounter on the way by night were largely professional bandits, who would almost certainly slit a man's throat for the value of his clothing – presuming, of course, that the bandits got him before the panthers, who were apt to be quicker off the mark. There were lots of panthers in the surrounding jungle he explained. So, if a man really collapsed and could not go on, another, fitter, man would be detailed to stay with him for the rest of the night, his job being to light a fire and to keep it going, this tending to discourage the panthers: but even two men, one of them very sick, would be no match for a bevy of hostile bandits, and every effort should be made to keep men with the column. With the coming of daylight, the need for the fire disappeared, and the fitter man would have to abandon the sick one and go ahead to rejoin the column at the next staging-camp, leaving the sick man to be picked up and put on a stretcher by the next party coming through. If we ourselves came across men from earlier parties, abandoned by the wayside, we likewise should put them on stretchers and carry them forward.

Again the Nip made the suggestion that once the journey was over and we reached our ultimate camps all of our troubles would vanish: but this was smelling more and more like an empty promise designed to buoy us up and keep us going, and to make those men so sick that they could scarcely move, strain every aching muscle and nerve to go forward, thus saving the Nips the trouble of intermediate casualties and getting as many of us as possible through to the final destination.

No one really believed the stories of throat-slitting bandits or of panthers, but all the same we realized that sick men left untended would have a rough passage: so back we went to our groups to exhort our troops, and soon we had shaken the dust of Bampong from our feet in exchange for the far dustier dust of the road to Kamburi.

For me, and for the small minority of our party who, like me, were reasonably fit, the march was unpleasant – at times decidedly unpleasant: but for the vast majority who were far, far, from fit, it was unmitigated hell.

A wide variety of factors combined to ensure that the memories of that march will live forever undimmed in the minds of 6,000 men. Only 6,000, for although between them H Force and F Force set out from Bampong 10,000 strong, slightly over 4,000 died within the next seven months – died from either disease or from common starvation – before the shattered remnants once more crawled into the rice trucks back at Bampong and were taken down to Singapore again.

Foremost, at the outset, was the plight of those many

men who were sick before we had even started, bearing all the real suffering of the earlier stages: but dysentery strikes quickly, and with new cases developing almost hourly, men who with only a little normal care and proper drugs could have thrown it off within a week or so were reduced to the final extremities.

Three of our men had had to be carried out on stretchers even from Bampong, and on that first night another half-dozen collapsed *en route* – when our six stretchers were full the others staggered along with one arm around the shoulders of each of two stout companions, one on either side, and we got every one of our party into the staging-camp.

So far as our party, at least, was concerned, the probably mythical panthers went hungry.

In spite of the 'easy pace' set at the front, the column straggled out over miles. Truck-loads kept together, but the pace was set not by the group in front but by that of the slowest member of each group, and if a man with dysentery had to hop sideways into the bushes it was no good the group keeping going and telling him to catch up – the chances of his being able to run were remote. The whole group had to wait. Altogether there was a gap of nearly three hours between the time the head of the column reached the staging-camp and the last remnants trickled in.

Having been told (mercifully) by the Force Commander that we should have to do our own cooking, we had juggled the truck-loads a bit and got the cooks up near the front. The cooks (surprise! surprise!) were amongst our fittest men: and after a mere half-hour rest on arrival they were set to work getting the cook-house going. The cook-house itself was in existence, with rice and water boilers, some sacks of rice and some sacks of yams, and several felled but not chopped-up trees. Job number one was to chop up the trees (we'd made sure that the axes and saws were with the early truck-loads), and in a very short time our cooks had got fires going, had collected water from the school well, and were cooking our much-needed breakfast.

The advantages of being near the front of the column

became apparent. Not only did we get our meal as soon as it was ready, but we could catch up on some sleep. Those near the back of the column admittedly got a meal immediately on arrival, but got it some two hours later than we did, and had two hours less sleep to look forward to.

As we had been warned, there was nothing like the bustling bazaar as there had been at Bampong: but there were a few odd natives selling mangoes and bananas, hot sweet coffee (which was very reviving), and one or two with charcoal fires in battered biscuit tins making omelettes. I had an omelette, and felt better.

For the second night, we made one slight alteration. On the first night, on the instruction of the Nips, Monty, Pat, and I had marched at the head of the column 'setting the easy pace', and indeed we three had had it pretty easy. The two MOs at the back of the column had had a dreadful time.

Not only were they on the road for three extra hours, carrying their own kit like the rest of us, but they had had to attend to the 'fall-outs' as they caught up with them and render what little medical assistance they could. But the 'fall-outs' had not all been wholly genuine. A number of men, faced with their turns to carry the communal kit including the stretchers (the trucks were all running a rota system to give the carriers stints of around half an hour), had fallen out rather than take their turns; whilst others had done so merely to grab a rest or even had had the idea that spending an hour or so on a stretcher carried by others was preferable to marching themselves. The MOs had had the unenviable task of trying to sort the wheat from the chaff, so that they could concentrate upon the really sick. Furthermore, on their belated arrival at the camp, they had merely grabbed a quick meal and then spent the rest of the morning doing their medical duties for everyone already there and needing attention before they themselves got any rest whatsoever. Both of them were completely flaked out, although one more so than the other.

For the second night, it was arranged that Monty and Pat should continue at the head of the column, but that I should accompany the fitter of the two MOs at the rear, whilst his less fit colleague should march incognito with one of the intermediate truck-loads.

My job was to act as 'whipper-in', and it was quite the foulest job which, up to that time, I had ever done in my life. Our arrangement was that as we met every fall-out, the MO would say 'leave this one to me', or else he would say 'this one's for you', meaning that he felt that my one was probably merely a malingerer, and that it was up to me to get him on his feet again.

The malingerers did not always stay by the roadside. If they were hoping for a ride on a stretcher, they did: but some had the idea that they could probably gain a whole twenty-four hours' rest if they could evade our column and wait to rejoin tomorrow's column. They realized that by doing so they would miss tomorrow's meal – but if they had a few hard boiled eggs and some bananas with them, this seemed tolerable.

As a result, I was obliged not merely to look at those on the roadside, but to poke around in the surrounding bushes and even flush out little off-shoots and gullies; altogether I reckon that for our 15-mile trek I did at least a third of it three times over – up, back again, and then once more up again: and all the time I was being haunted by the nagging suspicion that I might be hounding on suspected malingerers who in reality were quite genuinely in need of the doctor.

During the first night, our preoccupation had been with those who had left Changi already sick, and with the explosion of dysentery: but now, as the second night wore on, we were having more trouble in numbers, if not in seriousness, with 'bad feet'.

'Bad' they were. 'Boots' was a mere courtesy-title for some of the flapping conglomerations of leather, canvas, rubber, and cardboard which the majority of the men had tied around their feet. Few boots had seen a cobbler for eighteen months, including the campaign prior to our capture followed by heavy months of heavy labour pulling the trailers in Singapore or squelching in the sub-jungle undergrowth felling timber: by no means new when they started and now reduced to crumbling ruins, with stitches burst and the uppers flapping, heels worn to the welt, and soles if not patched with bits of motor-tyres cracked across or holed right through to the bare foot inside.

'Bare foot' it was, for socks or stockings, other than wrecks like shabby lace, were a rarity: and bare feet, in ill-fitting broken-down boots are not to be seen at their best marching through the tropics without even water to wash the feet at times.

Blisters – big blisters – were forming rapidly, and equally rapidly bursting and filling with dirt, soon to turn septic and hurt ten times worse: in consequence a pitiful host of otherwise fit men were limping along with their truck-loads with open, weeping, bleeding sores that were rubbing and growing worse with every hobbling step they took, and not a few of them eventually falling out and joining the rabble at the rear.

Our rear-end rabble grew. There was nothing that the MO could do for them, and so it fell to me, as 'whipper-in', to shepherd them along in an increasingly resentful, muttering, mob. They repeatedly fell out again and hid in the roadside bushes, and I was kept hopping about like a mad marionette flushing out both sides of the road and stirring them up and all the time grimly forcing them ever and ever forward, trying to ensure that none was missing and that all were still in front of me.

Coaxing, ordering, threatening, swearing, driving them on to exertions far beyond their capacity, to many of them I appeared clearly and understandably as a lustful, sycophantic satellite of the powers behind this devilish fantasia: but less than a 100 yards behind me stalked the Nip guards, and although I might lash the men with my tongue, those who did slip past me and were spotted found that our hosts were addicted to far more concrete goads – the boot or the rifle butt.

Much as I hated it, I had to do my job.

My whole idea of leaving nearly all of my kit at Bampong had been to travel as lightly as I possibly could, thus increasing my chances of survival: but the effort was poorly rewarded, for all night long I found myself carrying at least one straggler's pack, and often two or even a kit bag or some other awkward bundle, giving the more exhausted of the cripples half-hour 'breathers' before handing them back their loads as others, even worse, began to flag.

Visions floated irritatingly before my mind of all of my own stuff, lying there in the dump, when I might just as well have been carrying it instead of the stuff of these other fellows: I silently cursed the inexorable law of Providence which seems to rule that the foolish virgins always get the laugh on the wise. They certainly had it here, for after the whole of the H Force had passed through, the Bampong dump was thoroughly looted, my bed-roll being amongst the things which were never seen again: and although some other people were eventually reunited with their kit, I was left with the clothes I was wearing plus the contents of my two light haversacks.

A bright feature – about the only bright feature – of that second night was the appearance towards dawn of some Thai hot sweet coffee and banana vendors. While on the metalled road we were still within the bounds if not of civilization at least of habitation; and the itinerant vendors had come to expect us. Although we were running short of money, they were more than welcome.

We got there at last, still leaving the panthers hungry, with our whole party intact.

8   Kamburi

The metalled road went as far as the ancient walled village of Kamburi, but our camp was some 2 miles short of it, at a small hamlet (called a 'kampong' in the Malay lingo) which straddled the road. Our camp was on the right-hand side, and consisted of a loosely fenced-off compound of shrubby bushes, but no trees, containing a tiny village school in use as the cookhouse, and half a dozen small tents housing very sick men from the parties in front of us. We had the bushes, or the open air; and the midday sun being pretty hot, the bushes were our prime choice.

We were ordered not to cross the road, but just behind our compound were six or seven attap huts housing a medley of Thais, ducks, chickens, pigs, and a few skinny cattle. It was here that we found the well from which water could be bought at five cents a bucket. A constant queue of a dozen to twenty men with pails or kerosene tins was keeping the delighted owner dishing it out as fast as he could pull it up.

The final rabble of our column had not got in until 11 a.m., by which time the front had already been in for several hours, and so we immediately got a meal: but we were quickly told of the facilities available from the little kampong behind us. In addition to coffee and bananas, they had a bath! This sounded like the next thing to heaven: so, having eaten I went along to inspect it. It looked less like a bath than a small cattle-trough, consisting of a small rectangle of four low brick walls, the oblong in the middle measuring about 5 foot long by 18 inches wide. The floor was covered with rough concrete, with a little hole in the middle for the water to get out when not secured by a bung of rather-grey rag.

The drill was that two of you clubbed together and paid ten cents each to get a shared four bucketsful of water, and then one sat on the wall at either end scooping up water with the half coconut-shell thoughtfully provided by the management, to remove the worst grime. One then got out, whilst the other knelt down to have a real wallow, scraping his knees, toes, hips, shoulders, and elbows on the rough brick sides and the concrete floor, but nevertheless revelling in every moment of it. You were allowed five minutes for the pair of you, timed meticulously by the impatiently waiting queue – but to us it was a bath quite unrivalled by that which one could get at either the Hilton or the Ritz, and I am sure that those two establishments will fully forgive me for saying so. I have stayed at many fine hotels, but I have no lasting recollection of the magnificent bathrooms of any of them. I shall never forget the Kamburi bath though.

The bath was just next to the well-head, and was supervised by the owner pulling up the water, whilst his wife was doing a roaring trade moving up and down the queue selling food and hot coffee. She had the usual small 'wok', a sort of two-handled frying-pan with a rounded instead of flat bottom: but this sat very comfortably on top of the inevitable large biscuit tin in which there was a small charcoal fire. She was selling fried eggs or omelettes, but nothing so elaborate as a mah-mee.

Meanwhile the daughter of the house, aged about fifteen (which is just about right for a Thai girl, as they bloom early and fade like the sunset, being 'old women' before they are thirty) spent most of her time leaning languorously against a mango-tree up near the well, with a most enticing smile on her lips as she watched the sahibs taking their baths, seeing what visible effects upon them were caused by her slit-to-the-upper-thigh sarong. Every now and then she would disappear for maybe ten minutes and then return, no doubt slightly richer but looking just as attractive.

Next door to our camp, back towards Bampong, was a

coolie forced-labour camp, with a high bamboo stockade. Armed Nip sentries with fixed bayonets were clanking about at the gateway whilst others patrolled the perimeter. We, the official prisoners of war, had no fence and no wire, and not even a sentry on duty to see that we didn't cross the road – a rather remarkable contrast, clearly bringing out the complete reliance placed by the Nips on distance and our conspicuous shape and colour as the true bar to anything in the nature of attempted escape. Coolies, on the other hand, could melt into the populace.

At about 5 o'clock came dramatic news. We were not to march out that evening, but would stay overnight where we were. A whole real night of sleep was wholly welcome, and after another meal, sleep we did.

On the following morning we received further orders. We were all to undergo a formal medical inspection, up at the Kamburi hospital 2 miles away: but that would not be until the afternoon, and so we had a free morning.

We had been told not to cross the road to the larger kampong, but our guards were not apparently concerned, and firstly a few and then a stream of us were across. This place was infinitely better than the cluster of squalid little hovels around the five cent well: the natives were obviously expecting us. They had even put out a number of tables and stools, and such delicacies were available as meat omelettes, fried mah-mee, fruit, coffee, and lime-juice.

We'd almost become accustomed to having terrific thirsts, for although we could have purchased a whole bucketful of water for five cents, it wasn't safe to drink, and the bottle-neck was the almost total absence of pots in which to boil it. Lime-juice at ten cents a pint was therefore really attractive as a means of getting a pint of boiling water, for the limes (of which one got three to the pint) were on sale elsewhere at one cent each; but money being increasingly precious, after one or two ten-cents' worth each, a group of us clubbed together and bought a bag of limes and a pound of sugar, and went back across the road to brew up a few cheaper gallons in a borrowed dixie.

Whilst we were still over at the main kampong, we

prowled around and found that there was another well at the back for which we didn't have to pay. Many men took the opportunity of washing their travel-stained clothes, spread them out on the ground and waited, stark naked, whilst they dried in the sun – they were as stiff as boards within twenty minutes. Whilst Bill and I were in this somewhat immodest condition we heard a small commotion at the front of the kampong. Nobody took the slightest notice of naked bodies, but our clothes were still drying, and leaving them unattended would be inviting their disappearance: so I was left to guard the clothes whilst Bill went forward to see what the excitement was about.

He rapidly returned, and told me and the others around the well that some men had come across the road with some well-nigh unbelievable news. The Nips had announced that they proposed to start issuing us with pay, in Thai money, and would do so weekly starting today. Furthermore, they would pay us at twenty-five cents a day, instead of the one dollar a month which we had had at Changi. Twenty-five cents may not sound much, but to our eyes it made Croesus look like a pauper: things seemed to be looking up.

The promised pay issue materialized. A week at twenty-five cents a day should have produced one tical seventy-five: but to our delight the Nips were short of small change, and they gave us two ticals each explaining that this would cover eight days, but that next week the pay would only be for six days.

There were still no orders to move, and we were to stay where we were for another night: so, after our formal meal of rice and pumpkin stew, many of us trooped across the road for yet another feast of mah-mee or omelettes. Three of us – Pat, the senior MO and I, improved the shining hour by finding a smelly little hut at the back where some natives were running an illicit still (forbidden by the Nips) and after a much elaborate palaver and overdone secrecy we at last got a bottle of their home made hooch for only two ticals. Raw though it was, tasting rather like a mixture of varnish and extremely cheap gin, taken with plenty of sugar and limes it could have been worse: and this being our first drop of alcohol for over a year, the three of us, back at the camp, got quite noisy and quite pleasantly heady. What it did to our livers, I would rather not think about.

The next morning we went for a swim in the river. The country, all the way back from Kamburi to Bampong, had been a flat plain, and we were now at only just above the height of the river. The road had roughly followed the river, and now we found that at Kamburi, there was also a railway, apparently following the same route. The river was quite close behind our camp, the railway was beyond that, and the road of course was where we were. The swim in the river therefore presented no problems, but was very, very, welcome.

Soon after we got back, a new Nip officer arrived and said that he wanted a hundred men who could drive trucks. At one stage the words 'ammunition trucks' were mentioned, which didn't particularly appeal to me, and I warned my own Signals personnel to be cautious: but by chance we had a contingent of the RASC (the Royal Army Service Corps) within the party as a whole, and they, together with a number of other volunteers (excluding my Signals) fell in and were marched off. We never saw them again until we met up with them at Christmas, seven months later, on the return train to Singapore.

I cursed myself then, for my advice to my own men. It turned out that the drivers had not been used on ammunition trucks, but solely on ration trucks – one of the cushiest jobs in the whole of Thailand where they fed well and didn't lose a single man dead in the whole seven months.

They marched off, and our party was thus reduced from 600 to 460 – the other forty having already fallen by the wayside – but when on the third evening that residue fell in ready to march on, we were kept waiting for three quarters of an hour and then the Nips told us that there had been another change of plan. Instead of leaving tonight, we were to leave at dawn tomorrow, and although it sounded too good to be true, we should be going by train instead of on foot. Four hundred men only were required, to travel in two batches, and so sixty of our sickest men would be left at Kamburi: although a handful of stubbly shrubs fell somewhat short of the ideal for hospital accommodation, we'd plenty of men who'd be far better off there than going forward any further.

9   Travel by Rail

The extra night's sleep was welcome for its own sake –
although the Adjutant's fierce muttering as he had to alter
up his nominal rolls by the light of a piece of string acting
as a wick in a jam-jarful of oil marred the first two hours.
At half past six we despatched our morning pint of rice,
the first group of 200 sallied forth headed by Monty, whilst
Pat and I were left to bring on the second group at half
past eight.

The station was just over a mile from the camp, but we
marched to it with something approaching a swing
compared with the awful shuffling rout that had prevailed
since Bampong, the sickest of us having been left behind
and the rest of us thoroughly rested: when we got there
the Nips led us to a string of open ballast trucks standing
at a siding, and bade us get aboard.

They were big, high-sided wagons, full to within 18
inches of the top with coarse gravel. With the whole train
of a dozen to fifteen trucks at our disposal, we spread
ourselves well out and took plenty of room. In we climbed
and there we sat until a little after noon, with nothing
much happening except all of us slowly growing hotter
and hotter.

The sun rose higher, and the heat, beating up in
reflected waves from the shingle, made us sweat like
stallions; the sole hot sweet coffee vendor to put in an
appearance disposed of his entire stock in one fell swoop
between the first two trucks at double the normal price –
we had money!

Working in the yard was a gang of other British

prisoners, and several managed to slip across for a chat when they knocked off at lunch time. We gave them the news from Changi, and they gave us theirs, telling us that they'd been up here in Thailand for eight months, having come up with one of the early 'overland working parties'. They had to work fairly hard, but with reasonable hours and good food: and certainly to look at them, they seemed pretty fit.

All work was tied up with the building of this railway, the big Nip project on which all previous overland parties had been engaged since they came up from Singapore. A single-track, purely military line linking eastern Thailand with Burma, was being built almost entirely by prisoner of war labour, supplemented by parties of impressed coolies brought up from the now idle rubber plantations in Malaya.

It started at Non Produk, a junction just north of Bampong, where it left the old established Singapore-Bangkok line and struck out north-west across central and north-west Thailand. From Kamburi it roughly followed the river we were now alongside, the Me-Nam-Kwa-Noi, climbing up the mountains adjacent to the ever deepening ravine, until it reached Three Pagoda Pass, where it went over the Burma border down the upper Ataran valley and then across towards the sea, to link up with the existing Burma rail system at Amherst, south of Moulmein.

When completed, it would link Burma to all the other railways of south-east Asia, for a new stretch eastwards of Bangkok had already been built to Indo-China; and thus provide a route through which the Nips could pour in supplies to their armies in Burma, at present dependent upon the atrocious roads or the vulnerable sea lanes.

Only the first 70 miles had so far been laid, but this, being mostly across the plain, had been easy. All of the really tough part still lay ahead, through 200 miles up to Three Pagoda Pass and then down again for another 100 miles, all of it through uninhabited mountain jungle – although it might by now be somewhat less, as the Nips were thought to be building eastwards simultaneously from the Moulmein end.

To this little history we listened with mild interest, for

incredibly thick-headed we seem to have been on looking back, our simple, trusting minds failed completely to grasp its true significance.

Here we were, a party stiff with sick and convalescents, bound, so the Changi Nips had assured us, for prepared camps and good food. And here were the Nips, in Thailand, the country which God forgot to finish: wild, desolate, cut-off from the most elementary civilization, but through which the Nips were determined to drive their new railway. Yet still, in our child-like innocent simplicity, we guessed at no connection between the two proposi-tions, although Heaven knows our treatment over the past two weeks ought forever to have shattered our faith in the value of the Nips' word.

The missing link, of course, was labour. Labour *en masse* was required for the construction gangs, and prisoners of war presented a source which could neither refuse to work, nor go on strike, nor do anything whatsoever to demand decent conditions, proper hours, or anything else to protect their own interests. For the early gangs, the Nips had demanded 'fit men' for the overland parties from Singapore, but these had been used on the easy first miles across the plain from Non Produk. Now, they needed more men, and as there were not enough fit men in Changi they had demanded parties, fit or not: and we had clicked for the vacancy of construction gangs on the further sites up in the jungle and the mountains. F Force, having a higher proportion of fit men, was destined for sites up as far as Three Pagoda Pass, 200 miles away. H Force, with a higher proportion of sick, had only a further 60 miles in front of them, having already done 30 miles of their original 90 predicted at Bampong.

There we sat, drinking our coffee and gossiping happily, heedless of the knell being sounded by our early party colleagues: until just after noon a locomotive with one more truck arrived, hitched up to the front, shunted about for a bit, and finally got going.

Once we left the siding the oppressive heat was somewhat relieved by the breeze created by the movement, although the shingle where we weren't actually sitting on was still too hot to touch: we trundled gently along through the whole afternoon, gradually climbing and watching the level padi give way to densening scrub, then light bamboo, until this in turn thickened into heavy, gloomy, teak forest.

This was the second of our Nip-sponsored train trips, and although the twin evils of over-crowding and long duration were so far absent this time, several new features made it quite as foul in their own little way as the first major trip up to Bampong from Singapore the previous week.

Sitting on the open trucks, close behind the engine, we received the full benefit of its wood-fired furnace. Every time it was stoked great showers of sparks streamed back, covering us with red-hot charcoal and burning countless holes in our precious, irreplaceable clothes, finally setting fire to a truck load of wood faggots.

Pat and I were riding on the second truck, and these faggots were on the first truck, the one which the engine had brought with it. We'd turned our backs like storm bound cattle to the fiery deluge belching from the engine, so we didn't notice the local blaze until it had a firm hold – so firm, in fact, that it had spread to the framework of the truck itself – and our first indication of anything wrong was when flames licked up and wafted over to our truck, mingling with the red-hot engine sparks which were singeing our backs and destroying our shirts.

We were travelling at only about 10 miles an hour, but the newly constructed track was so shockingly bad that we rolled and pitched and lurched about like a cockleshell in a tempest. The idea of leaping nimbly from truck to swaying truck to merely quench a fire and save a bit of Nip property dazzled neither Pat's eyes nor mine: and so we just sat tight and bellowed at the driver to try and make him stop.

The line was being operated, as well as just built, entirely by the Army, and so the driver and the stoker were both ordinary Nip soldiers. Our shouts gained their attention and made them look round, so we waved our arms and pointed to the smoke and flames. They slowed down, stopped the train, grabbed a shovel each, jumped down, and raced back.

So far, so good: but when they reached the fire, instead of climbing aboard and getting to work they ran straight past it and ignored it altogether, and came up to and clambered aboard our truck. Then, without the slightest warning or explanation, they turned on Pat and me and proceeded to beat us up with their shovels for all that they were worth.

Pat had a stout walking-stick, with which he unwisely tried to parry the thudding hail of blows to his head. The driver seized it and poked him in the belly with it with considerable force: whilst I, having grabbed the stoker's shovel in an attempt to put him out of action, was being kicked on the shins to such effect that I had to relinquish my hold.

Wielded by a demented savage, a shovel can be quite a nasty weapon, but we knew too well the reprisals likely to follow anything but passive resistance: and so there we stood, the pair of us, for a long, long minute, looking rather silly and being knocked even sillier at the inexplicable whim of these two little yellow devils.

There was no sign of their stopping, and so we, feeling it high time that the action was called off, started to retreat, backing slowly away across the shingle to the far end of the truck, warding off with our arms and dodging as best we could the continuing attacks of the two yelling maniacs following us up.

Meanwhile, two of our Guards had collected shovels from the engine and had started to deal with the fire, throwing out the burning logs and then smothering the flames where the body of the truck had caught fire, whilst another Guard brought a bucket of water from the engine and brought the operation to a close. Our attackers grudgingly put up their weapons and stood back, glaring and snarling like two thwarted dingoes: and there, as was so gallingly usual, the matter ended. There was no higher Nip authority on hand to whom we could appeal: there'd be no one later on to listen to complaints. As the driver and the stoker spoke no more English than we did Japanese, nothing could be done on the spot in the way of explanation. With a few final angry grunts and cries of 'Bogero' (a word we came to hear frequently, and which we understood to mean rather what it sounded like), our assailants returned to the engine and the train got under way again; whilst Pat and I were left to unprofitable speculation as to just what it had been that had this time disturbed the inscrutable mind of the Orient. The most likely answers were that either they reckoned that we ought to have climbed over and put the fire out ourselves, or they may have thought that we were trying our hands at a little quiet arson – presumingly losing our nerve halfway through, unless they had mistaken our shouting for a gloating paean of triumph. Whichever of the dozens of equally stupid possibilities had clouded their tiny minds, we thought very little of their methods of sorting things out.

The next bit of excitement arose over a hill. We chugged round a curve and came in sight of an unusually steep gradient: but in spite of a rapid dash and much puffing and blowing we failed to make it, and the train came to a shamefaced halt only about halfway up.

We backed down, waited to get up steam, and then took it at a run: but we still failed to make it and so back we went for a third shot.

This time we reversed for a whole mile, to enable us to get up speed. We waited whilst the engine got up so much pressure that it was spouting hissing jets of steam at every outlet; and then, with loud tootings of the siren and a shower of sparks that peppered my hat until it looked like a part-worn colander, we charged forward, round the bend and up the hill with a mighty rush, rocking about from side to side like an automatic waist-reducer.

Still, for all the hissing, hooting, clattering and clanking, we only got about three quarters of the way up before we ground to a halt; and so the Nips, losing faith in the power of steam and in teak logs, issued the orders 'All men out. All men push'. They could not carry on a conversation, but they had learnt the English for various essential commands, and now used two of them. Their command of grammar was poor – they should have said 'All men *off*', as, on top of the shingle, we were already about as 'out' as we could have been: but the message was clear. To the greater glory of Nippon as exemplified by the skill of her surveyors and of her construction engineers, we at last reached the summit powered by one engine and two hundred prisoners.

All went well for another dozen miles, but then, about an hour after sunset, the train stopped again, and round about in the inky darkness we heard the voices of many coolies. Their presence was soon explained, for they swiftly surrounded the trucks, and without warning they pulled out the retaining bolts which held up the sides.

Each side was in one complete piece, hinged at the bottom, so as they flopped down, the ballast, suddenly released, shot out carrying us and all of our belongings with it down to the ground. Down we slid in a slithering scree of cascading shingle – packs, gravel, haversacks, men, waterbottles and mugs, all mixed in a swearing tearing tumbling swirling avalanche, to the excited squeals of the coolies, who had not guessed at our presence.

We scrambled to our feet, gathered up our bruised selves and such goods and chattels as were attached to our persons, and then groped around in the darkness and probed in the gravel for all the loose kit. Much of it was half or wholly buried, and the fact that the night was as black as the devil's waistcoat cut our chances of finding the more widely-scattered stuff to zero: I personally was lucky, having only my two small haversacks hanging from my shoulders, but many others lost a whole lot of their looser items such as hats, mugs, etc., and even Pat's ill-fated walking-stick had to be abandoned in its dark pebbly grave.

The Nips were impatient to get on. They had delivered their ballast to its destination, but they still had a further part of their journey to complete. The sides of the now empty trucks were bolted up again, we were made to climb in, and the journey resumed once more, with us wondering whether after all it was such a great improvement upon marching. Marching was pretty grisly, admittedly, but once it was over it was over; whereas nothing could restore to our Sergeant Major his lost and buried waterbottle, nothing could restore to Pat his stick, and nothing could repair the innumerable burns in my and many another's shirt. And when, with a tremendous crash, a tropical thunderstorm burst about our ears, we cursed long and loud and reckoned that our cup of misery was about full.

We shivered and shuddered, our teeth chattering like castanets above the screaming of the elements and even above the insistent clamour of Pat bemoaning his lost stick: until at 10.50 p.m. we drew into a siding and jolted to a halt, to be told by the Nips to get off and to board another train which was standing alongside us.

The moon was just rising, and we found that we were at what had obviously once been a small railhead, with several sidings and stacks of sleepers and rails, now very muddy in the aftermath of the storm (it had by now, mercifully, stopped raining). We squelched across to our new train, which consisted of only three lower-sided trucks and a very small engine such as one generally sees shunting about at the docks or at an engineering works.

Three open trucks seemed a trifle tight for 200 men, for as in Malaya the Thai railway was only metre-guage – but the Nips had said 'in' and so in we all got, with men sitting on the edges all around and the rest standing up in the middle – there wasn't room enough to sit. Those sitting around the edges did so facing inwards, as there was nothing to hang onto if one faced outwards, and it was a pretty precarious perch. Facing inwards, you at least had your legs firmly pinioned by the mass of legs of those standing up.

The engine gave a feeble little 'peep-peep' on its toy-like whistle, and off we went on the next lap, firmly convinced that 'travel by rail' was the slogan of an idiot.

I was in the first truck, sitting on the edge, with a view largely of other people's trousers or lack of trousers, but my legs safely confined by their legs: the only time that I glanced around for a glimpse of a wider horizon, I hastily turned back, wishing sincerely that I hadn't done so. We were passing over a wooden viaduct spanning a 100-foot ravine, and as the truck was slightly wider than the sleepers, and there was no hand rail let alone a parapet alongside the track itself, there was nothing whatsoever between my overhanging rump and the rippling water shimmering so prettily below in the moonlight.

I refrained from looking again, and for the rest of the trip confined my gaze to the vista of jiggling trousers: half an hour later we came to a great sprawling tangle of sidings hemmed in with enormous piles of sleepers and other constructional stores. The hoarse cries of the Nips bade us get off again.

It had started to rain again, and we formed up in a dripping, dejected column for the Nips to count us. This took longer than necessary, owing to one wretched troop having crept off behind a pile of sleepers for admittedly understandable purposes, but without having the sense either to obtain permission or to warn his neighbours: but at last he returned, got clouted by the Nips, and the numbers tallied. We set soggily off along a narrow mud track.

It debouched shortly into a wider, but equally muddy road, churned up into deep ruts (being merely trodden-on and wheeled-on earth with no foundations or metalling), and flanked closely on either side by the thickish forest of which it had recently itself been part.

We trudged through the slush behind the Nip Guards for some while. The road forked and branched in several places, and numerous little tracks led off into the wilderness at the sides: with the Nips pausing ominously at every major turning, it soon became obvious that they hadn't the slightest idea as to where to lead us. After nearly an hour we came to a crossroads which we were sure we had visited before – we had been round in a circle.

We took a different branch this time and trudged on. We passed several clearings and what looked like camps, but they were all utterly dead and did not look as though they were meant for us. The rain was easing up, but we were cold and tired and hungry, and when the Nips showed signs of giving up and spending the rest of the night where we were by the roadside, we began to get Bolshie.

We managed to urge them along, our Japanese-speaking prisoner who acted as our interpreter risking his neck by pointing out that even if the Nips couldn't go on, we could: and eventually we came to a Nip guardroom, with a lamp alight inside, and heads visible through the window.

Our Nips were most reluctant to go inside and confess that they were lost: but our intrepid interpreter (he spoke only the minimum smattering of Japanese, but it was enough) stepped forward to the guardroom doorway and beckoned to them. He was seen by the Nips inside, one of whom came out, and our own Nips had sheepishly to go in with him.

We could hear them being cursed for fools inside (which didn't bode well for what would happen to us later): then they reappeared, turned our column round and made us march for 300 or 400 yards back the way which we had come, and then turned off onto a minor track. A few hundred yards along this, we came to a place where the trees thinned out, and there was a number of blazing bonfires.

This was indeed our camp, and the bonfires belonged to Monty's first 200 train-load. The camp, as we'd come to expect, consisted simply of an allocation of semi-cleared jungle, with no shelter whatsoever from the elements other than the trees and the more lower-lying bushes. It was even worse than the two previous camps, for on this occasion there was no school for use as a cook-house or tents for a hospital for the sick. Mercifully, we had few sick, having left the worst behind at Kamburi and not having acquired many during our train ride. The rest of the ground was pretty grotty. The whole place was running with water and dotted about with treacherous patches of grass-covered bog onto which you could unknowingly tread – in fact it was exactly as one would expect to find a semi-cleared forest towards the end of a very heavy storm.

There was no food, and Monty had been told that none would be available until the morning. We'd had nothing to eat since breakfast the previous day, before leaving Kamburi, and it was now nearly 3 o'clock in the following morning: so with bitter thoughts on the ability of the Nip administration, we sought the only bit of comfort which we could in crowding around Monty's bonfires.

At around 7 o'clock, by which time it was light, a Nip truck drove in from the far end of the camp. It contained not merely sacks of rice and pumpkins, but also two huge woks, each about 6 feet in diameter, and weighing what seemed to be about half a ton. However, our noble cooks soon had them up on mud ramparts and got fires going underneath, and by 10 o'clock we had a hot meal. After that we had a rest, and then we had another meal at 2 o'clock, and began to feel better.

We had been told that we should march out at nightfall; and so in the afternoon Bill Shakespear (he spelt it without the final 'e') David Eastham, and I, with several others, went down to the river for a wash.

Our camp, on a level with the railway, was considerably higher here than it had been at Kamburi, and it was quite a walk down to the river. However, when we got there it was quite a busy place. There was a jetty and even a crude attap warehouse, and we encountered some old acquaintances who had come up from Singapore the previous year on one or another of the early overland parties. They told us that this was Tarso, the present construction railhead, a mushroom village which had sprung up from nothing purely for the purpose. The main railway only went as far as the little railhead where we had changed trains the previous night, with heavy trains only going as far as that whilst the final section was really just temporary, bringing in materials for the work ahead. The temporary line only came up as far as Tarso, and there was no track beyond here, merely site-preparation.

The men whom we met observed that they were now having it easy. They were the sick who had been left behind when their parties had marched on up country over the past few months; but this being an organized base, they were now sitting pretty, doing no work, and being more or less left alone. Food in their part of the camp down here by the river was quite good, being brought up by barge and including plenty of vegetables and occasional meat issues. The warehouse ran a canteen, and as they were still being paid they could buy eggs, biscuits, fruit, and tinned fish.

We wished them sweet dreams, bought a dozen eggs from the bargee of a barge which had just come in, and took them back up to our camp to boil them and take them with us when we marched out. The meat, the eggs, and the fruit were evidently peculiar to the jetty area, for none reached our camp up the hill, where our rations were strictly rice and pumpkins, and not too many pumpkins at that.

Short of the top of the hill to us were Australians. H.3 had marched out of Bampong one day in front of us, and had been one day in front of us up to Kamburi. From then on, however, they hadn't come by train, but had marched forward to Tarso in three stages. They had arrived a day before us, and were all, not unnaturally, far more exhausted than we were: the Nips had very generously said that they could have an extra day's rest, and instead of marching out again last night, they were to march out tonight, along with us. We, of course, having had the dubious luxury of coming by train, did not need an extra day's rest: but at least we had avoided three whole nights of marching.

10 Through the Jungle

That night's march, although not our last, was quite unlike those going before or after, and was an episode on its own.

The Australians went first, coming up the hill through our camp to join the main road along which we had arrived, and they left whilst it was still just light at 6 o'clock, we being scheduled to follow two hours later at 8. To add to our manifold joys, as we were rounding up the troops to get them in column, the heavens repeated their previous evening's performance, turning on every nozzle and dropping it down by the bathful.

It was by now pitch dark, for the moon was not due to rise until midnight, and even the starlight was blotted out by the heavy rolling clouds: our only illumination was the fitful glare of a bonfire which we had built by the track, but even this was now being shrouded in thick smoke as the rain pelted down on it.

One of the Nip guards had an electric torch, and this, with the fire, enabled us to form up: the roll call miraculously agreed, and we set out on what was to prove to be the most nightmarish march which it is possible to conceive.

Once we were round the first corner, the light from the bonfire was lost, and so apart from the lucky few nearest the leading Nip, no one could possibly see anything, absolutely and literally.

The first corner proved to be the junction where we had turned off from the main road that morning down the little track to our camp. We now turned left on that main road, past the Nip guard hut where we had gone in for directions, and then on. This was evidently the road up through the jungle.

The road itself was merely beaten earth where lorries and marching men had nosed their way through what was fairly light jungle, un-made, un-metalled, and in no way planned. Smaller trees and secondary vegetation had been cleared, but large trees had been left and the track simply wound round them. Every few score yards there were twists, turns, and right-angle bends; and as no attempt had been made at levelling the track, it rose and fell with the frequency, but not the smoothness, of a switchback at a fun fair.

Superimposed on these minor undulations was a longer trend. We were gradually climbing, but the track was running crossways over a series of ridges and dips about a quarter of a mile from crest to crest, and we came to stretches with gradients of one in six, one in five, or worse, with a side-slant for good measure, and sharp detours around larger unfelled trees for even better measure.

Such was its shape – not easy to follow in pitch darkness, and incomparably more tortuous than any woodland track or cliff terrace I've ever scrambled about on in England: but far more exhausting than its layout was its surface. Once the protective carpet of ferns, roots, grasses and other low-growing plants had been removed, the floor of the track consisted of soft, crumbly, black, moist, and exceedingly rich soil, the humus of the decaying vegetation of the ages: and walking on this is rather like trying to dance about on a well-dug flowerbed.

No doubt it had been quite bad enough before yesterday, but now that the monsoon had broken (for we found that the previous night's downpour had been the onset of the full season) the entire track, or 'road', was reduced forthwith to a slippery, snaky, treacherous quagmire.

On the level stretches the liquid mud was now inches deep, covering the whole surface so that ruts and potholes were equally concealed, and a step taken might just as well land in a foot-deep rut as find something solid to contact a couple of inches down, whilst in the valleys a seemingly-innocent little puddle could as well be 2 feet deep as 2 inches.

On the hills and on the crests, the loose top-soil was rapidly being washed away, laying bare a harder strata of packed earth and small rocks: but this, with a thin covering of the sea of mud which was still being eroded, was even more slippery, and we found that we were losing our balance and falling over the whole time.

Blind as bats, but without their in-built radar system our only hope was to keep a hand on the man immediately in front, and also to rely upon any shouted warnings from him: but although you could feel him and hear him, you couldn't see him, and any errors which he made you were almost bound to follow. The road would take a turning, but in the darkness men would stumble straight on, falling waist-deep into the side ditches (where they existed), or tripping into the ruts and, top-heavy with the weight of their kits, sprawling head long.

Within the first few miles Pat, who had a magnificent pair of riding boots instead of standard army boots, but which in consequence had no studs on the soles, had been down twenty times – no gentle topples but hard, painful falls, sometimes forwards and sometimes backwards as he slipped on the steep muddy hills or tripped on hidden boulders. Few of us had manged to avoid half a dozen at least, stumbling up to our knees in the ruts and pitching flat on our faces, twisting our ankles, cutting our hands and knees to ribbons on the sharp flints, knocking the breath from our already well-nigh exhausted bodies, and getting covered from head to foot in the clammy, clinging sludge.

It was so completely dark that often a man would fall, and three or four others close behind him would trip over on top of him; and a mass of fighting, struggling men would themselves slither into the ditch, lashing out, screaming and cursing, losing their kit in the pitch darkness, unable to see a thing and losing their temper with the remaining shreds of their self-restraint and self-control.

By midnight, we had covered only just over 4 miles in as many hours' marching, and the column had stretched out for over a mile in little blobs: from then onwards the pale gleam of the moon (it had stopped raining), in spite of the seething obscuring clouds, at least banished the chief terrors of the crazy blind man's buff that had been our chief tribulation. Light, however dim, meant sight, to however small a degree, and cut out the worst dangers of floundering into the ditches, crashing into the piled-up trunks of felled trees that lay along the verges, or, in the more open patches, even of wandering right off the road.

Of course, there still remained the hills and the rocks and the mud and the slush, and in many of the dips and valleys young ponds had collected at the bottom, the depth of which was mere guesswork – and if the road took a chance twist, then only even luckier guesswork coupled with the fate of the man in front, could avert a slip and a ducking. The muddy liquid surface and the liquid muddy potholes on the flatter stretches were difficult or impossible to distinguish: we still kept falling into the ruts and falling over on the slippery hills. The night seemed never-ending as we plodded wearily on and on.

Whenever we halted for a rest, our soaking clothes chilled us in a moment and clouds of rapacious mosquitoes flocked around us and bit us to distraction, eager to give us whichever variety of malaria they happened to be carrying: even so, although we restricted our halts to ten minutes at a time, I twice fell asleep where I had flopped down, from sheer fatigue.

Fairly early on a Nip truck had come up from the back and passed through the column, frequently having to be helped through ruts and potholes by pushing by the prisoners; and another one came through in the early morning, similarly assisted. Evidently they hadn't cottoned-on to what the monsoon was already doing to the track. We caught up again with this second one just after dawn, lurched heavily sideways in the ditch, and abandoned by its driver.

About an hour later we came, to our almost frantic relief, to a prepared camp which the Nips announced as being our destination.

The relaxing joy with which we hailed this news was soon ruined, for as we entered the gateway the first swift impression of the camp revealed so much as to prick the bubble in double quick time. Set in a minute clearing, with a tall bamboo stockade which rather pointlessly only ran around two sides, it was no more than about 50 yards across and maybe 100 yards deep. A swampy little 'square' of churned-up mud occupied the foreground, a number of tents and two extremely home-made attap huts lined the periphery, whilst just by the gate, on the left of the square an open-sided smoke-wreathed cook-house crouched in dismal squalor beneath a rough matting shelter.

The camp was already occupied, and bunched on the slushy square, the party in occupation was just getting on parade. They were drawing what was evidently a 'haversack ration' of a mugful of plain boiled rice apiece with a morsel of dried fish which we could smell from where we had come to a halt on the road outside: within ten minutes they were all marched off, out along the road, in small squads each with a Nip guard – but they were not carrying their kit.

We stayed where we were, and the British Camp Commander came out and painted a somewhat gloomy picture. He was very decent, and set some of his men to building several bonfires on the square in front of which we could try to dry ourselves off; and he had already ordered his cooks to brew up some hot tea for us. But that was the limit of the good news.

His men had not been marching off to another camp, but merely to their day's work, and would be coming back tonight, and so this camp could not be scheduled to be our ultimate destination. However, dysentery and malaria had been cutting enormous swathes in his own ranks in the last few weeks, and he thought it highly probable that the Nips intended us to provide reinforcements for his working parties. When we shook our heads and observed that less than thirty per cent of our party were now fit for heavy duty, he smiled a wry smile and looked at us pityingly as one would look at an unsuspecting child. 'Fit to work' in Thailand, he explained, was something quite different from what we had been accustomed to in Changi. Here, the Nips made all men work unless they were actually bedded down in hospital, and there was no such category as 'fit for light duties only'. Either you were prone in hospital, or you worked.

Meanwhile, that was a hurdle which we had yet to jump – the immediate problem was where we were to go. This camp was already full to overflowing, and we could not see either another one or some extension.

Through our interpreter we asked our Nip Guard Commander. Yes, he informed us suavely, this was indeed our final destination, and we were earmarked to reinforce the present dwindling party on a constructional job on a rock cutting, about a mile distant: as for accomodation, that was the simplest matter of all. If Monty followed him, he would show him where to go.

Stalking out into the roadway again, with Monty, Pat, me and our interpreter behind him, he squelched along for about 200 yards, stopped, took out a piece of chalk from his pocket, and marked a tree with a large cross. Fifty metres long, he said, and 100 metres deep: the sooner we got busy and cleared the jungle and built a camp and a cook-house, the sooner we'd get some sleep and have a cook-house in which to cook ourselves a meal.

And so here we were – Eldorado at last. The 'camp in the hills, where sick men could recuperate'. A random patch of untouched, untamed, virgin jungle, with dense bamboo clumps, denser undergrowth, soaring trees and matted creeper, dripping and running to swamp already with just the first two days of the new monsoon: and only our own exhausted, tottering, hungry troops to call on for labour as they dribbled slowly in, dead beat, from that purgatorial 12-hour march.

The author, after
evacuation from Dunkirk

The author (centre) with
Captain Forbes on his left,
and Lieutenant Eastham,
rekitting in Ceylon on the
way home, after the
liberation of Singapore

The interior of a typical prisoners' hut in Thailand

Prisoners of war on the westward march in July 1943. Marching
by night was worse

A prisoners' working party in the jungle

Typical attap huts

A well-earned rest, with the rails laid and the section completed

Prisoners of war after work on the Burma railway – victims of Japanese atrocities in Thailand

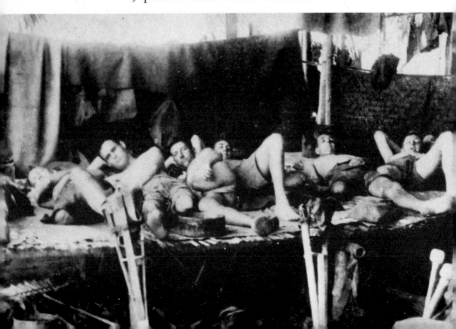

An elevated view of a prisoner-of-war camp

Inside a British prisoners' hut. The space allotted to each man was 75 centimetres wide

Two British and three American prisoners of war awaiting repatriation after the liberation, February 1945

June 1943: British prisoners of war lay sleepers ready for the
rail-laying party

British prisoners of war in June 1943 put down rails transported
from base on flat trucks

Prisoners at Kamburi line up for a meal

Crosses marking graves at Upper Canu

11 One for Every Sleeper

Arguing would be pointless. If this was what the Nips had decreed, this is what we should do.

The men carrying the axes and saws had been up near the front with the cooks, ready to prepare firewood: we now set them to work on the flattest looking piece of scrub to make it available as a cook-house. However, we pointed out to the Nip that firstly we had no rice or anything else to cook, and that even if we had we had no utensils in which to cook it.

Resourceful as ever, he demanded a working party of eight men, and marched them back to the camp across the road. There he commandeered four sacks of their rice, and two of their large woks – much to the chagrin of their camp Commander: but he assured him that the woks would only be on loan, as woks and supplies of food were on their way up from Tarso by truck.

This, actually, proved to be true. The eight men came back across to us with the rice and the woks, and our marvellous cooks had a meal going before the tail end of the column got in. But just up the road beyond our new camp was a Nip truck, evidently one of those which had passed us during the night – the Nip told us that this one carried tents for the camp, not food or cooking pots. We gradually unloaded it and brought the tents back: but the food and our woks were evidently on the second truck which had got stuck in the ditch by the wayside.

The tents were pretty pathetic. They were standard Indian Army tents, consisting of the outer tent proper with an inner flysheet, but at some time in their pretty lengthy history they had obviously been folded up and stored while wet, the result being that the fabric had inevitably rotted, and one good pull on a guy rope or one sharp poke with an elbow led to a split seam or another gaping rent in the middle of a panel.

Only two were provided with pegs or poles, and for all the others we had to find suitable bamboos or saplings, lashing ridge poles and strengthening the guys with lengths of tough creeper. The Nip guards appropriated one of those with poles and had it erected properly with tent and flysheet: on counting the rest, we worked out that by using the flysheets as tents by themselves, we had one to approximately forty men. Each was 12 feet long, and they were meant to take eight men, giving 3 feet of shoulder space to each man, or for twelve men at a pinch on active service, meaning only two feet of shoulder space. Between forty men, it would mean only 7 inches apiece, which would be ridiculous; so we split the men into parties of forty, and told them to work out rostas amongst themselves whereby twenty of them would sleep inside and the other twenty in the open on alternate nights. Two of the main tents, being of tougher material than the flysheets were allocated to the doctors as a hospital.

Shortly after noon the plight of the second truck was revealed to our Nip Commander, the driver being in the camp across the road where he was recovering from being beaten up by his colleagues for having abandoned his truck: and a working party of a dozen men was sent back to push it out. They did, and just before nightfall it arrived with our own woks and supplies of rice and what turned out to be radish-tops. We had already fed on our neighbours' rice, and so our new goodies were left until the morning.

By the end of the day we had made substantial progress on the building of the camp. The bulk of the ground had been cleared, the tents were up, the latrine had been dug, and the cook-house had already given us that second meal: but before we turned in for the night, the Nips had us all out on parade for a roll call.

Men had been dribbling in all through the day, so we

were not over surprised that, when we were counted, we were still three short. Not so the Guard, however, and as usual their wrath fell not on the missing men themselves, but on the nearest people handy, to wit us. After a lot of unpleasantness, particularly for Monty and for Bill, we were told that we should have to send out a search party to look for them. *We*, mark you, not the Nip guards were to go out: but we'd grown so accustomed to the queer Nip mentality that it seemed perfectly natural then, and the utter incongruity of sending out a party of prisoners to round up another batch of prisoners occurred neither to our captors nor, at that time, to ourselves.

I, having a good pair of socks, had come out of the march with my feet in relatively better condition than most others, so I said that I'd be the sucker; and two of my own Signals officers, David Eastham and Jimmy Weir, volunteered to come with me. The Nips wanted us to set out at once, but we pointed out that as it was dusk already, and would be pitch dark in half an hour, we shouldn't stand a cat's chance of picking up the stragglers, and would quite probably get lost ourselves into the bargain: at last they reluctantly agreed and we were permitted to wait until dawn next day.

We duly waited and then, after nine hours of blissfully heavy slumber, we stoked up with a good breakfast of two pints of rice each, and set out back towards Tarso.

In daylight, we could see where we were going and see our every step, thus managing to avoid nearly all of the worst pitfalls; but even so the road was more like a mud bath than a highway, and we'd just had about enough when, 7 miles back, we at last ran our quarry to earth, finding, to our immense relief, all three of them together.

They were sitting on top of a lorry – a Nip lorry, part of a small convoy of ten heavily piled ration trucks – and we, thinking how nice it would be to ride instead of tramping through the too familiar mud for another 7 miles back to the camp, clambered up and took our places beside them, explaining to them with some acerbity just why we had had to come on our not very welcome trip.

As we'd anticipated, they'd fallen out with bad feet on the first night, spent the first night in the jungle, but were now coming along under their own steam perfectly well – so our quest, as we had expected, had been absolutely pointless. They had marched a few miles yesterday, but whilst having a rest they had been overtaken by this convoy, and the Nip driver had actually waved them aboard.

In a very short time we discovered how serious an error we had made in joining the convoy ourselves. The road, bad as it was to walk on, was now far worse for lorries, and they slid into ditches, wallowed in the ruts, and ploughed enormous furrows with their sumps and rear axles: they stuck at the bottom of all the major hills with monotonous regularity.

If a hill was not too steep, and one truck got stuck, the drivers of all the other trucks would get down and come along to push. Our three men with 'bad feet' were not made to help, but we three who had come to look for them had been met whilst walking, and so obviously were 'fit', and were made to help the 'pushers'; we came to regret ever having joined the party.

For the really steep hills, they had with them a guntractor, with caterpillar tracks. It didn't just tow them separately, but went on ahead to the top of the hill and then winched them up one by one with a long cable.

The second time that this happened gave us our chance. We had tried to get away earlier and walk on by ourselves, but our driver, seeing part of his main motive power disappearing, had called us back and had since kept a pretty close eye on us.

Now, fed to the teeth with our unpleasant impersonation of a yoke of oxen, we took the opportunity whilst our driver was engrossed with steering while being hauled up, to slip off into the jungle and we eased our way along until we came out in front of the convoy around a sharp bend and out of sight, and by walking we eventually reached our camp a whole hour before the mechanical wonders caught up and passed us.

By the time that we got there, the building of the camp was fully finished: this meant not only the erection of a lamentably few square yards of dilapidated canvas over a patch of new-won jungle, but also the construction of a top for the latrine, a matting and bamboo roof for the cook-house, a place for ablutions by the edge of a little stream (which ran parallel to the road, but about 50 yards back so that it was not too contaminated), and floorboards for the tents.

These floorboards followed the design of Chinese or Nip 'chungs' – little raised platforms covering the whole floor except for a narrow aisle down the middle, raised up about 12 to 18 inches from the earth floor. The idea was that you could walk in in your muddy boots, tramp about in them down in the aisle, and then, taking them off, climb up onto the chung and keep everything up there clean. Highly effective, in point of fact! On the chung you kept your blanket, and all of you slept in a row just as you would on the floor of a proper building, whilst underneath you could store your boots, and any other kit.

We had made the chungs from split bamboos. To a European, 'bamboos' are probably pretty little clumps in the garden with the shoots about as thick as your finger. Here, the shoots were up to 6 inches in diameter at the base, and rose up to over 40 feet, but split and beaten flat they made slightly springy although extremely rough and knobbly planks: and bamboo variously dealt with served us for nearly everything.

At the edge of the stream – it was only a tiny brooklet, but flowing fast and thus reasonably clear – Monty had had three large sumps dug: the top one for the cook-house and deep enough for buckets, the next one nicely revetted with slats of bamboo, for clothes washing, and the lower very large one as a communal bath and ablution centre.

Apart from the latrine (with its bamboo slats across the top), those three sumps constituted the sum total of our camp's civilized amenities; and now that it was complete and the Nips had given us two whole days to 'look after ourselves', we were due to go out and start work the next day.

They allowed us a total of twenty men to run the administration of the camp, including Monty, the doctors, the medical orderlies, the cooks, and two wood-fellers to keep us in firewood at the cook-house. The remainder, apart from those already bedded down in the hospital (including Pat Malins, who had had a really terrible journey) were split into three companies, labelled A, B and C; and then each company was further split into three squads of about thirty-five to forty men, each squad having a British officer in charge. Each man was given a little bit of white cloth bearing a Nip character and a letter and number in English which we had to pin to our hats; and I, being the Senior officer and in charge of A Company as well as number one squad, was labelled 'A.1', which sounded rather superior, whilst poor Jimmy Weir, being the third officer in C Company, was somewhat unfairly stigmatized as 'C.3'.

Once we were all decorated, we drew a pint of rice each with a little bit of fish, to carry in our mugs or mess tins (we had earlier had our breakfast); and we were led out by some Nip engineers rather than by our own guards to commence our first day's work.

They led us for about half a mile on the road back to Tarso, and then we turned off right, down a narrow track that kept branching and splitting into yet narrower pathways: although, being at the very front, I did not know it, down each path a separate squad was led, and when we arrived at the workplace I only had squad A.1.

The jungle had been thinning out for the last 100 yards or so, and we quite suddenly came to the crest of a bluff from which the vista was quite breathtaking. We were on the outside bend of a promontory above a great wooded valley, across which a line of hills similar to our own formed the other side about 2 miles away. Up-stream a couple of sharp bends meant that our view in that direction was limited to the brilliantly green tree tops of the jungle in the valley: but to our left one could see right down towards Tarso and Kamburi, where the misty purplish blue of the distant mountains mingled softly in the shimmering haze with the lighter, mistier, powdery blue of the sun-filled vault of the sky. Below, occasional flashes of silver scintillating from the steaming forest betrayed the snaking Me-Nam-Kwa-Noi as it wound down to the plains. It was truly beautiful.

When we looked down over the crest, the beauty ceased to enthrall us. The railway, or rather the bed for the railway now being constructed, was climbing up round the edge of the range on a series of narrow ledges, cuttings, and slender timber bridges; at our point it was some 20 to 25 feet below the crest of the ridge, and ran through a cutting of about that depth and some 12 feet wide across our small promontory. At the eastern end was a gully about 20 feet wide, and some rough scaffolding indicated that this was going to be an earthfill to connect it to a tricky looking ledge already hewn in the face of the next cliff: whilst to the west there was quite a deep ravine spanned by a half-built wooden trestle bridge leading to a cutting now being hacked out in the next promontory in that direction.

Much as we had enjoyed gazing for a few minutes at the spectacular scenery, before we had so much time as to get our bearings, our vista was forcibly limited to the scorching, glaring, yellowish-brown inside of the cutting which had been just below us. We were led down into it, and were promptly set to work without more ado on our task of helping to blast and clear out the rock.

A party which we discovered came from the camp across the road from us was already there in a little bunch, drilling holes 80 centimeters deep into the solid rock of the cliff face with 12-pound sledge hammers and long steel chisels to take charges of dynamite; lying at the far end, where last night's blasting had loosened the rock, a great mass of boulders and rubble was waiting to be cleared.

This was to be our job, but 'loosened' was a comparative term. Everything which the Nips considered to be remotely 'loose', we were now made to shift. Firstly, we got rid of the small crumbly fragments, carrying them in small wicker baskets – flat, shaped like a dust pan but about 15 inches across – up to the eastern end where we tipped the contents over into the intended earth-filling. After that, we carried the medium-sized rocks in our arms and tipped them over, and finally we scraped at the seemingly bare surface, looking, with picks and crow bars, for any cracks which might indicate boulders which could be prized up, muttering unanswered prayers that there would be no cracks to find. When we did find a crack, we had to worry at it with the picks and crow bars, and

eventually get the boulder out and lever it along to the end
of the cutting and tip it over into the gully. By the time we
had finished, the floor of the cutting was completely solid,
with no loose areas.

In the narrow chasm of the dust-filled cutting, with the
sun (this being May) directly overhead and beating down
on the parched, bare earth, it was sweating stifling work:
but although we worked there for ten long days, and ten
long hours every day, neither the work nor the hours
irked us to anything like the extent as did our overlords.

Eight of them, seven privates and one full Corporal,
stalked up and down the cutting with stout staffs of
bamboo; and their ideas of the best methods for ensuring
our maximum efforts and also of our capacity for work
differed widely from our own.

The wicker rubble-baskets, being 15 inches wide, had a
handle at either side rather than one in the middle like a
dust-pan, and as they were quite heavy when filled, we
put two men to a basket, one at either side. This did not
suit the Nips, who very soon ordered 'one basket, one
man'. They then watched to see how we were operating.
We had one man with a pick, digging bits out, and he had
another man as a 'shovellor' who collected the bits and
shovelled them into the baskets. This meant that the
basket-carrier stood idly by whilst his basket was being
filled, and so the Nips ordered 'one man, two baskets'. He
would leave his recently emptied one to be filled whilst he
took the full one over to the gully, and when he got back
the empty one had been filled again, and he could tote it
off to the gully without waiting.

The man with the pick was getting a short breather
whilst his shovellor gathered up the loosened debris and
filled a basket: and so the Nips now insisted that a man
with a pick should work two faces. Whilst his shovellor
was collecting from face one, the man with the pick
should attack face two, and so his pick was constantly
swinging up and down without a moment's respite for the
whole day. We partially overcame this by making the pick
man and his shovellor switch over every now and then:
but neither of them got any rest, even when changing
jobs.

The slightest sign of any easing up, even for the momentary purpose of wiping the streaming sweat from out of your eyes, would bring you, should you have been so unwise as to do this whilst a marauding Nip was near you, a resounding crack with his bamboo on the head, the legs, the shoulders, or the face: and if you even more unwisely faltered more openly, you could get a full-dress thorough beating-up.

The first sign of approaching major trouble, such as was likely to occur if a man was only carrying one medium-sized rock when a Nip opined that he might have been carrying two, or if an unskilled city dweller was using the wrong end of his pick, would be loud shouts and cries of 'Kura!', the Japanese equivalent of 'Oi!' or of 'Hey, you!'. This would be followed by a high-speed babble of Japanese, and then when nobody carried out whatever the instructions had been (no one having understood them), an even more impassioned outburst would follow, built up mostly around the word 'Bogero', the meaning of which we *did* understand. It meant 'cretin' or 'dolt' as well as what it sounded like.

The bewildered victim, still failing to grasp the Nip's meaning, either did nothing or, worse still, did the same thing again which had precipitated the diatribe: and the Nip, in a frenzy of furious rage, would begin lashing out with his bamboo or whatever tool happened to be handy, and would carry on until either he tired or the Corporal in charge came and took over.

The Corporal was a swine of the first water, his favourite punishment being to stand his victim on the very brink of the ravine holding two 12-pound hammers or a crow-bar at arm's length over his head for up to two hours. As soon as there was the slightest sign of sagging at the elbows – and 25 pounds at arm's length is not frightfully restful – the game was to kick him on the shins, or sometimes for a change in the groin, to kick his knees, or to slash his face with a bamboo switch, and then, as a titbit, to spit full in his face. And believe me, a great gob of Nip spittle feels none too pleasant, particularly when you can't wipe it away and have to let it trickle down until it dries off in the sun.

His subordinates joined in the game, and started doing it off their own bat, until they suddenly lost interest. One prisoner, realizing that he was going to fall backwards, managed to grip the shirt of his tormentor and took him with him, over the top to their deaths in the ravine far below. The Nips had not only lost one of their labour force and one of their own men, but they had lost two sledgehammers, which were in short supply. The practice stopped.

They had discovered an ingenious method of improving upon their bamboo staves. By splitting the end, it would, as it flailed through the air, splay out like an egg whisk: and then, when it hit you, the split ends all closed up together again, catching up little ridges of flesh and tearing off ribbons of skin with the sharp cutting edges as they pulled it gleefully away.

They then found a variant upon the 'cliff edge'. Just before blasting time, they would make miscreants stand with their sledgehammers or crow-bars above their heads up against the cutting face. The cry would go up for all men to climb out of the cutting up to the safety of the top of the bluff, but leaving the hammer holders where they were. The Nip corporal would go along setting light to the fuses of the dynamite charges, and then only when they were all alight he would shout the word 'Go!', and the hammer holders could drop their hammers and scramble out just before the charges went off. This amused the Nips enormously.

Ten days it lasted: and then, from the rock cutting, which was virtually completed, number one squad was moved to a new location, which was in many ways worse.

This was 2 miles the other way from the camp, which meant an extra march morning and night; and here the railway was just emerging from the cliff ledges and was swinging onto a fairly level stretch across the top of a high plateau. Our job was to dig the cutting from which it emerged, about 20 feet deep at the end where it started; and then it graded off over several hundred yards until it got up onto the flat.

Instead of solid rock, it was heavy red earth: but with the monsoon being nicely in its stride, shovelling the wet

and sticky clay was no mere flick of the wrist. We then had
to carry the earth (one man, one basket) up the sides of the
embankment. It was preferable to the dusty heat of the
quarry – in the mornings: but the rain would start up late
in the afternoon every day, and it came down like a
cloudburst for six solid hours, making the baskets even
heavier and making the little tracks up the sides of the
cutting ever more slippery.

Even so, it was better than the quarry: but there was a
tension in the air, the Nips were scanning their blueprints
and their maps, and we sensed with a feeling of dread that
the whole tempo of the show was noticeably quickening.

This came to a head on the fourth day, with a surprise
visit by a Nip Engineer Captain from Canu. Canu was the
big camp 3 miles further on, and this character was the
Engineer-in-Charge for construction for the whole area.
For the Nips, a captain was very high ranking indeed –
had this been a British operation the place would have
been bristling with full Colonels and Brigadiers – and he
carried considerable clout. He had paid us one fleeting
visit before, at the old cutting, but nothing had come of it:
and this time, as he strolled along inspecting various
groups of men at work, he again looked quite peaceable.

My squad was working at the deep end, and so he
reached me last: the Corporal, who had been busy
badgering us, didn't see him coming until he was right on
top of us.

From a distance of about 6 feet the captain gave a loud
shout, and the corporal spun around, leapt to attention,
and started evidently apologizing.

The Captain cut him short, and asked him several
questions in a normal voice. It seemed quite a happy little
party, but at one answer the captain's face (never very
pretty) clouded in an angry scowl. His tone harshened, his
voice grew louder, swelling up and up until he was
shouting at the top of his lungs; and the Corporal,
standing rigidly to attention, became almost silent,
reduced to muttering an occasional miserable 'Hai!' at
irregular intervals.

As his anger increased, the pillar of the Samurai stooped
down, grabbed some clods of earth and stones, and hurled

them at his subordinate who, standing at almost arm's reach, received them full force: finally the captain lurched forward and laid into the Corporal with his stick, knocking him over and kicking him hard where it hurts most as he writhed on the ground.

Delightful as it was to see our tormentor tormented, we, as the pygmies, knew who was likely to suffer in the long run when the giants fell out: and sure enough, when the Captain's outburst had spent its force and he had stalked off, the blitz on us started in earnest.

Much has been written about the supreme importance to the Oriental of the matter of 'lost face'; and our Corporal had lost enough face by his treatment in front of us to last him for a lifetime. He lost no time in re-establishing himself as the big noise, passing on all that he had received with bountiful interest: and I, as the officer-in-charge, came in for a generous share.

My job here was that of being 'number one', a sort of glorified ganger and fetcher and carrier of tools and ropes and what-not from the dump. I stood on the parapet rather than down in the cutting, and was meant to see that the men were hard at work: but although this meant less physical labour for me, it carried with it the doubtful privilege of carrying the can for any failures within my squad. Every day various men would come in for a bashing, and when several did it on the trot, I'd get one too for failing to prevent what had gone wrong from going wrong.

The Corporal was aware that I was also acting as a look-out, easing the men off whenever his back and the backs of his roving colleagues were turned, and giving the warning to look busy when one of them approached.

He disliked this, and was no man in whom to instill a personal prejudice; he frequently objected that I wasn't driving the men sufficiently, and that I wouldn't beat them. Every now and then he would come along and give a little pantomime portraying me gazing vacantly heavenwards and motioning to the men to take it easy, then peeping over my shoulder at the Nips and springing to life and shouting a warning as one of them approached.

This would be followed by a demonstration of the 'right

way', the corporal leaping about and shouting at the men and plying his bamboo liberally: at the end of which he would fetch me a crack or two and shout 'You no good. Me number one'. I would then be demoted, and would descend into the cutting to get on with shovelling, whilst he would take over the direction of operations from the parapet.

Today, as part of the programme of recovery from 'lost face', it was indicated to me with cries and wallops that I was a Bogero of the very first water, unfit to be a number one and fit only for a shovel: and down I went in the deepest disgrace whilst the storm gathered momentum.

All down the sector, as we discovered from other squads when we got back to camp that evening, the growing repercussions of the Captain's wrath were causing minor eruptions – it was not only in our sector – and that afternoon, with the Nips yelling and bashing like maniacs, we sweated as we had never sweated before in our lives.

Our lunch-hour, which had normally been for a full hour, was cut down to 25 minutes. Our 15 minute 'tea-break' at 4 o'clock (it was a water break actually, as we hadn't got any tea) went unrecognized; and at half past six, our usual knocking-off time, nothing happened and we continued working.

At 7 o'clock I arose from out of the pit, found the Corporal, and pointed to my watch. He waved me back to my shovel with a cry of 'Speedo!'. I tried again half an hour later, to be met with the same cry of 'Speedo!'; and at my third effort at 8.15 p.m. the repeated cry of 'Speedo!' was accompanied by a couple of whacks around the head with his bamboo.

On we toiled, practically dropping from fatigue and extremely thirsty, until at 9.20 p.m. when it was too dark to see, the Corporal grudgingly sent the cry of 'Yasumi' echoing down the line.

We stumbled over to the tool dump, where the Nips seemed even worse than usual at slugging fellows who hadn't cleaned every scrap of mud off their shovels, or who piled them in sixes instead of the statutory five; and then we found, to our disgust, that instead of our going straight back to the camp for a hot meal, the meal had been sent down to us, which meant that it was no longer hot and we had to eat our cold boiled rice and radish top soup shivering in the rain.

By the time that this was over, and the tools checked and we ourselves counted, it was past ten, still pouring with rain, and as dark as the bottom of a disused coal mine: but the Nips had a little generator, which lit two somewhat feeble floodlights, and we ate our meal and handed in our tools by that glimmer. But by the time that we were due to go home (home! – ha! ha! – but we always referred to the camp as 'home') we could no longer see where we were going, and were reduced once more to relying on sounds and the sense of touch.

Bad as the road had been a fortnight ago, it was now infinitely worse. The monsoon had made it a patchwork of swamps and little riverbeds, with the slopes too slippery to stand on, let alone climb, and the smooth sea of liquid mud making the 2-inch deep ridges look identical to the 18-inch ruts. Wheeled traffic had stopped using it altogether, apart from a few lumbering ox-carts toiling through to Burma, to the obvious discomfort of the oxen; and all of our rations were now coming up the river by barge, which entailed a 3½-mile carry by us to the nearest jetty at Lower Canu.

Going to work in the morning daylight we didn't use the road itself, but we had beaten little paths through the jungle running roughly alongside: but now, on the dark way back from our first day of the 'Speedo', with the moon again on the wane and the starlight blotted out by the monsoon clouds, we couldn't possibly risk getting lost on these little twisting tracks. The only practicable way of progress, we found, was to get into a rut on the road and then wade blindly along it, with the sludge up to and over the knees, frequently slipping and sometimes falling headlong, completely submerged, but keeping direction by the high sides of the rut, which prevented one from straying.

Coming as the finale to a 15-hour day, that fiendish 2-mile trek every evening really was the finishing touch. I say 'every evening' for from this first day forth the 'speedo' went on for a whole fortnight, with us parading at 6.25 a.m., working until 9.30 p.m. or later, and getting back to camp at anywhere between eleven and midnight – for the man who could cover those 2 miles home in under an hour was a superman.

The 'speedo', we learnt from the Camp Guards (not the Engineers who accompanied us to work) had arisen because our sector was behind schedule. One answer would have been to draft in more men to the labour force, but not only had the Nips no extra labourers readily available, but with our rapidly increasing sick list, the existing effective labour force was rapidly dwindling. The only answer was to make those still capable of working work longer hours. The fact that this could well eventually kill a number of them off through being denied medical care didn't matter – if you were going to have a man die in a month's time you had at least had two or three extra days' work out of him *now*. If every sleeper laid on the railway cost another man his life, so what? 'One for every sleeper', but the railway would go forward, you would have your extra sleeper, and all that you had lost was an expendable and extra useless mouth to feed. Logical, if a little cruel.

Several times men who tried to get back to camp without sticking to the ruts got lost, and spent the rest of the night in the open jungle, seldom reaching camp in time for breakfast (served in the dark at six), and joining up with the parties on their way out to the cutting to avoid the inevitable bashing if they failed to turn up, had empty stomachs for the first six hours until lunch time on their day's work.

Even if one did get in, it was no great joy, although the sleep that one did manage to get was pure unalloyed heaven.

Half asleep already with the ovewhelming exhaustion, you staggered in at somewhere maybe around 10.30 p.m., washed the mud off by sitting down exactly as you were in the sump in the stream – you were always covered in mud as it was virtually impossible to get back along the ruts without falling at least once – and then hang your sopping clothing on the tent ropes and crawl into your place (if you were lucky enough for it to be your place on the chung, or if it was your turn to sleep out, you stayed out).

Six or seven hours later – although it seemed more like six or seven minutes – you'd be woken again, draw on your still soaking clothes (how I loathed that!), then file past the cook-house for your morning breakfast of a pint of rice plus a further pint of the filth in your mess tin for lunch.

There, in the cook-house, lay the real core of our whole trouble.

Even the working hours, even the intensity of the labour down in the cutting, even the appalling conditions under which we were living in a handful of tents in a morass so recently cut from the jungle: all of this we could have borne and more if only they'd given us proper food.

The official daily ration was 20 ounces of rice, uncooked, with a little salt and a small issue of dried radish-tops, enough only for one soup a day. We had plain rice for breakfast, plain rice for lunch, and rice and radish-top soup or 'stew' for dinner: but not only did the radish-tops taste utterly foul, they played such havoc with many men's bowels that many couldn't eat them.

After the first few days we also got dried fish – but only for the workers. Those bedded down in hospital didn't get it: but the quantity was such that even the workers were not over-nourished. The ration was one fish between fifteen men, and as the fishes measured about 10 inches long including the head and tail, it only worked out at one decent mouthful of fish per man.

Even tea – the love of Europeans – was missing: as we had to boil all water to make it safe for drinking we usually drank it hot and pretended that it was tea. And so if, like about fifty per cent of us you had the squitters and couldn't take the radish tops, all that you had to eat, day in and day out, was three pints of boiled rice and one mouthful of fish.

The result of this, quite naturally, was semi-starvation. If you bent over too quickly, you blacked out and fell over. You grew weaker and weaker and men started cracking up right and left although for no apparent reason; and vitamin deficiency, on whose borderline we'd all been now for well over a year, cut growing swathes in our ranks with beri-beri and eye troubles.

Apart from diet troubles, living as we did without mosquito-nets or drugs in the jungle, the inevitable happened, and by the end of the first month we were riddled with malaria. Dysentery, brought with us or contracted on the way up from Singapore, was still spreading: and worst of all the sick men simply couldn't recover.

The only drugs which we had were the few odd scraps which the doctors had brought up in their packs – brought on their backs at the expense of their own personal kits – plus those two small panniers, and a trifling quantity of quinine which Monty had squeezed out of the Nips as the malaria was spreading.

The quinine was enough as a palliative but not for a cure; emetine and M & B tablets (the name of which derives from May & Baker, pioneers of the sulfa and sulfanilomide drugs) for the dysentery were non-existent; and we hadn't even rice-polishings or palm oil for the deficiencies. Once a man managed, or rather, if a man managed to get over the climax of his illness, the minimal diet of plain rice, with or without the doubtful addition of the radish-tops, was nothing like sufficient to build back his strength; and so instead of recuperating, once he went sick he probably just faded away.

There they lay, in the rotting tents, slowly getting sicker and sicker, many with two or even three diseases at once: and although as yet they weren't dying in appreciable numbers, the chances of their rejoining the active workforce was greatly hampered by the almost unbeliev-able attitude of the Nip Engineers.

Every morning our own little Engineer officer – not the captain from Canu, but a vicious little viper, whom we knew as 'Oswald' and was in charge of our particular subsector – would come into the camp himself during the morning and would conduct his own sick parade. The really fit men had already gone off to work, but he would classify all those remaining as 'bedded down' in the hospital tent, or 'fit for work'. Everyone who could stand up was made to come out on parade, and with no medical knowledge whatsoever he would swagger up and down 'classifying' everybody. He would wave a lucky few back to the hospital tents, would wave rather more to one side as being fit to go down to the cutting, whilst those left over were deemed to be fit for camp duties such as tree felling or ration carrying.

Having not the slightest shred of medical knowledge, Oswald went purely on what he could see. A big running ulcer or a thumb smashed with a sledge hammer would be likely to stand you in good stead, and might get you waved back to the hospital, whereas 'medical' cases, with nothing much visible, such as dysentery or malaria (unless you were in the middle of a rigor), would usually be condemned to the cutting.

Our natural response was to mark more and more men as 'bedded down' and to smuggle them into the hospital (Oswald's rule being that only those sent off by himself should go into hospital): but the rising figures called forth loud and venemous comment from Oswald each morning, until at last we sailed too close to the wind, and he put on the screw which we had feared most of all.

We'd reached nearly forty per cent of our total strength as 'bedded down', and after he'd created a scene and bashed the MO, this preposterous blackguard turned out every man in the hospital on parade. Out they came, many of them leaning on sticks or having to be helped or carried; and then, on a completely random basis, he went down the line picking out every third man, irrespective of his condition. Obviously, he collected a number of the most seriously ill men that we had. Further and renewed protests merely led to a further beating for our MO: and out the pathetic little band of seriously sick went down to join the working party in the cutting. A number of them passed out quite early on, long before they reached the cutting, but as soon as they came round they were driven on and were kept out all day working with the rest.

I did not keep an accurate note of how many of them died within a month, but it was several. Meanwhile, Oswald had met his quota of extra men for the day, and was no doubt satisfied. We still hadn't finished with

Oswald, but I am happy to report that, once the war was over, he appeared before the War Crimes Commission and was duly hanged.

This latest effort of Oswald's was what we had feared, and as far as we could see the only means of preventing a recurrence was by ourselves keeping the hospital figures down to a minimum, so that we, rather than Oswald, should decide who at all costs *must* be kept in. Men had to be *really* sick before they were bedded down.

Even so, our hospital figures were still rocketing, and two weeks after the start of the 'speedo' I had only five fit men left in number one squad out of my original strength of forty. As number one I had less physical labour to perform than did the men, save for when I was occasionally demoted: but by the end of the fortnight the hours in the cutting, the lack of food, and the general conditions combined with a tooth and a mosquito to lay me low too.

It started in the middle of a conference down at the cutting, the Corporal having assembled all the number ones to exhort them to further prodigies of labour by our men; and in the middle of his harangue I surprised both myself and my colleagues with a big unrehearsed act.

I'd been troubled for several days by a back tooth which had broken, letting out the stopping and exposing an awkward hole with an unburst abscess at the bottom. I had mentioned it to our MO, but he had cheerily told me that he was a doctor and not a dentist, and had neither dental equipment nor even a pair of pliers. So, unless I was prepared to borrow a pick-axe from the cutting, it would just have to rip.

It suddenly began aching in the middle of the Corporal's conference with increasing violence, working up to a pitch until I flopped down on the ground and threw a most spectacular fit.

My breathing got quicker and quicker until I was gulping and snorting like a winded hog, and then all of my muscles started to contract, my knees curling up to my stomach and my hands and arms coming up to my mouth like a dog trying to beg. My eyes rolled like a buck Negro's, and at last with a volley of gobbling gulps I passed clean out: the Corporal was so impressed with this unexpected performance that he had me put on a stretcher and sent back to camp.

I came to before we had even started, and the stretcher was still being made from a rice sack and two bamboos: but I lay doggo, having no overwhelming desire to remain where I was. The journey home started, but after only about 200 yards I came to the conclusion that I would be safer as well as more comfortable walking. The stretcher-bearers couldn't get firm footholds on the slippery track, the sack was only long enough to support me from the neck to the knees, and after they had dropped me in the mud twice, I got off and we all walked together. I started to apologize to the stretcher-bearers for being a nuisance, but they assured me that they preferred this to working in the cutting, and with luck would not be sent out again but would get the rest of the day and evening off. We got back to the camp, and as I was trying to explain to the MO what had happened, I obligingly threw another identical fit for him to see for himself. I threw three more during the afternoon, but apart from saying that it must be some nerve affected by my tooth, the MO could do nothing, and somehow it sorted itself out.

By the next morning I was still feeling pretty mucky, but my dear friend Oswald leapt upon me and decided that although not fit enough to go down to the cutting, I was quite fit enough for a ration-collecting party. We'd had several brushes in the past over various incidents, and I don't think that he liked me very much, and so the ration party it was.

This job was normally reserved for the more serious malaria cases – the less serious ones having gone down to the cutting – as a form of light duty; but involving as it did a trek of nearly 7 miles, for the homeward half of which two of you carried between you a sack of rice, 'light' was not a very good description.

The first mile was muddy, but the next mile and a half was comparatively easy, with the road not so swampy here, running along the top of a plateau. After that, a dizzy zig-zag wove for over a mile down the mountainside and when we eventually got to the jetty by the river, I was feeling feverish and was wobbling at the knees.

The climb back, taking 200-yard turns with another man carrying our sack of rice, weighing one hundredweight, was about as much as I could manage; but I struggled on for a mile or so on the flat and then I passed out by the roadside, and stayed out.

My companion covered me up with his groundsheet (it was raining hard, but I was so soaked already that it didn't really matter), and wisely left our sack of rice with me instead of trying to go on and carry it all the way himself, and went back to the camp. There he collected two more men, and they came back for me with a stretcher with the odd man carrying the rice: when they got me back the MO confirmed that I had collected a dose of malaria. As I had a temperature of 104.9°F, this qualified me for bedding down in hospital, and I was pretty ill for several days. Not for too long though, as after only three days the Nips announced that all 'fit' men were to move to a new camp further on, whilst our present camp would be left with one MO as a hospital only. The move would be made the next day, and not being 'permanently unfit' I had to forget about my malaria and gird up my loins for travel.

12   More Sleepers

Everyone was to move except those whom the Nips labelled as 'permanently unfit', which meant men who would still not be fit enough to work again by the end of next month, or who were unlikely to recover without evacuation to a base hospital.

'Fit enough to work' was of course 'fit' by Nip standards: and although our own MOs on leaving Changi had spoken of 'only forty per cent fit', this did not in any way tally with the Nip definition. We had left Singapore with 600 men, of whom 100 had been siphoned off at Kamburi as drivers or mechanics: and then we had lost a number of others on the first two days' march, and had left yet more at Kamburi, whence we had only had to take a level 400 on the train trip to Tarso. At our first working camp the Nips had considered the whole 400 as being 'fit for work' on the simple basis that if you were not fit, you would never have survived the march up from Tarso.

But that march, and the subsequent toil and the 'speedo' had indeed taken their toll. That I have not been over-drawing the picture was borne out by the fact that now, after only five weeks at the working camp, we had to leave 147 'permanently unfit' behind, and only 253 could go forward as 'fit, or likely to be fit within a month': over one-third of us virtually written off within five short weeks. Such was the effect of the 'speedo'.

It was only to be a short march this time, of about 8 miles: but with so many men sick now, but hopefully expected to be fit again within a month, the burden on the fit men was going to be considerable. Not only would they have to carry their own kits, but also those of the sick men too weak to carry their own loads, as well as those of some of the sick men too weak to march and having to be carried on stretchers. Mercifully, the Nips had told us that we should not have to carry our tents and the cooking pots, but that they would provide a truck for this purpose. It would not go alone, but would accompany us at the pace of our column so that we could push it if it got into difficulties.

We were to march by daylight instead of by night, even the Nips having realized the impossibility of our having to wade along the ruts in the darkness. We duly paraded at first light, after a ration of rice for breakfast, and with the tents struck and piled, and with the cooking pots stacked: but no Nip truck appeared. We waited all day, with no orders from the Nips to move: the remaining cook-house cooked us up some more rice, and we spent a chilly night waiting in the open, including the usual evening rainstorm.

Early the following morning the truck arrived, we loaded it up with the tents and the cooking pots, and off we set. It was very much better marching in daylight and using little trails alongside the road rather than the road itself: compared with that nightmare trek up from Tarso it was a cake-walk, albeit with a rather larger number of stretchers.

When we eventually arrived there, we found that our 'new camp' was merely an annexe to that of our old travelling acquaintances, the Australians. Not having had 100 drivers and mechanics stripped out at Kamburi, they still had the remnants of their original 600 train-party; but they had had crippling casualties – and the Nip idea was to amalgamate our two parties into one party working up to strength.

This sounded fair enough, until we learnt that the reason why the Australians were so below strength was that they were in the throes of cholera. They'd had it for just over a week, but it was spreading like wildfire, and already men were dying at a rate of four to five every day. Into this holocaust, without protection of any sort, with no innoculations and in the full knowledge that no drugs or serum and no hope could be given to any future victims, the Nips deliberately brought us up from a so far uninfected camp.

A few more days of work, and then death – so what? Another man dead, but another sleeper laid on that accursed railway – 'one dead man for every sleeper' – but all that mattered to the Nips was those extra sleepers.

The original Australian camp had straddled the road. The ground sloped quite gently from right to left, and a clearing to the right of the road had housed a few tents and the Nip Guard tent, this side of the road being rather drier and less muddy. On the left-hand side they had had most of their tents and the cook-house. A small stream ran alongside the road, and probably from seepage the left-hand ground was damper and muddier.

That was as it had been, but the Australians had reorganized themselves within the last couple of days. Tents had originally been allocated on a 'working party' basis, but now they had reorganized them on a 'sickness' basis. It was easier clearing down the left hand side, and they had extended their area by clearing space towards the bottom of the hill for two tents for cholera victims, as far away as they could get them, and with a trench filled with lime through which one had to walk to reach them, rather as one has a trench at the entrance to a farm which is in the throes of foot and mouth disease. The Nips had only produced the lime yesterday. Above the cholera tents were the dysentery tents, which smelt even worse but were on the right side of the lime. Then came the non-smelly malaria and beri-beri tents, and above those the 'fit men's tents' and the cook-house. The only remaining inhabitants of the right-hand clearing were the Nip guards, who preferred the drier ground.

We were allocated the right-hand clearing, but on the understanding that as and when we got infected by cholera, our own victims would go across and join the Australian cholera tents, and the same would happen with our bedded-down dysentery cases. We would also share cremations, using just one fire and a joint team to service it; but apart from those, we should try to keep the two camps as separate as possible to minimize cross-infections, and in particular we should run our own cook-house, the Australians warning us about the importance of having a separate little fire with a can of water constantly boiling next to the food-issuing point so that everyone could sterilize his plate or mess tin immediately before eating from it and before the flies and blue bottles could walk about on it spreading disease.

It did not seem too bad. The site was already cleared, a latrine had already been dug, and best of all when sending the truck for the tents from the previous camp they had given us some more tents, so we had enough for everyone, with no one having to sleep in the open. But there the good news ended. Having been marching for most of the day, we were told to produce a hundred fit men for a working party at 7 p.m.

Although there was no formal 'speedo' going on, with fifteen-hour shifts, the Australians had all along been made to work twelve-hour shifts, changing over at 8 a.m. and at 8 p.m.: but this meant that if you were on the night shift you couldn't get off it except by working for a whole twenty-four hours in one go, which had one very unpleasant consequence.

The work here was again on a rock cutting, about a mile from the camp and reached through the usual little track of churned-up mud. The shifts changed over down at the cutting, not back at camp, and so the men were paraded at 7 a.m. to be counted, and then had to march down to commence work at 8 a.m. The party coming off duty had to march back to the camp, and did not arrive until some time after 8.30 a.m. But that did *not* mean ten and a half hours for food and sleep. On five days a week rations had to be collected from the river, which involved going out at 1.30 p.m. and getting back between 5 p.m. and 6 p.m.

At our previous camp the ration parties had been drawn from the semi-sick, but here *all* men not bedded down had to go on the working parties to the cutting, and so the afternoon ration parties had to be found from the now off-duty night shift. A man would work or be going to and from work for the best part of fourteen hours, do a four-hour ration fatigue, and have only six hours out of twenty-four for feeding, cleaning himself up, and sleeping.

For the first week or so, when we still had over 300 'fit' in the combined Anglo-Australian camp, each individual only got two ration fatigues a week. It would have been even less, but of course one half of our 300 were on the day shift, and only the other half were on the unhappy night shift.

On three pints of rice a day, all this, of course, was impossible and flesh and blood could not stand the strain; and in addition to the overwork we had dysentery and other diseases spreading at a frightening pace. As the numbers of 'fit' men dwindled, the burden carried by the remainder consequently grew, until after only a few weeks the fitter men were doing all five ration fatigues a week as well as working the night shift in the cutting, and only having two days a week of real rest. As they gradually cracked up, more unfortunates, just past the crisis of their exhaustion or illnesses but in no way fully recovered, would be forced out in their place, lasting in their turn perhaps three or four days before they themselves had to be replaced by yet others not quite so ill.

Just as this gruelling programme put that at our previous camp in the shade, so did the new Nip Engineers make the last lot look like gentlemen. There, they had generally beaten only those whom they caught flagging or had somehow provoked their precariously balanced ill-humour; but here they beat up indiscriminately, beating every man in a gang if they wanted it to go faster, and two of them in particular were simply blood-thirsty sadists.

They were known to us as 'Musso' and 'The Bull', and they seemed to compete amongst themselves as to who could cause the most hurt. They were both on the night shift, and both would come on duty with a rope's end strapped to the wrist. These they plied liberally, and they also carried a split-ended bamboo apiece, whilst Musso in particular would lash out with anything which came handy, such as a shovel. Every morning two or three men would come back to camp with blood clotted on their faces and shoulders or matted in their hair, whilst others would return with puffy scarlet faces but no eye lashes or eye brows, these having been burnt off where they'd had a naked acetylene flare waved slowly across the eyes – a favourite trick of another Nip known to us as 'Snowdrop'.

They drove the men on, not just to make them work, but as a cruel master drives a beast of burden to force it on to further efforts greater than it can manage; and one would see half a dozen men staggering along with an 18-foot tree trunk, or rolling an outsize boulder to the edge of the cutting, with the Nip running alongside lashing out at them or kicking their knees and shin and ankles to keep them going.

Frequently men fainted, and to make sure that they weren't shamming, the Nip would kick them in the stomach, ribs or groin. If the man still didn't move, the favourite trick was to roll him over face downwards, and then jump up and down on the backs of his knees, so as to grind the kneecaps themselves into the loose gravel. If he fell on his side, a variation was to stand on the side of his face and then wriggle about, grinding and tearing his undercheek in the gravel: and as a way of telling a faked faint from a real one, both of these methods are, believe me, highly efficacious.

On one occasion a man was beaten up so badly by the Nips that they thought he wouldn't live, and so they got four prisoners and told them to bury him under a heap of rocks. The prisoners observed that he wasn't yet dead, but the Nips indicated that that didn't matter – they could bury him alive. It was only after a great deal of persuasion by a spunky Australian officer (who naturally took a personal bashing for his trouble, but didn't let that deter him) that the Nips eventually changed their minds and let the man be carried back to camp. He was carried on a stretcher, and came round later, but the beating had sent him almost off his head; he disappeared into the jungle and we couldn't find him for two days. On the third day he crept in for food; but he was now quite mental and became a gibbering idiot at the mere sight of a Nip. Had we bedded him down in a hospital tent, he could very well have simply popped off again; and so we found him a job in the cook-house where he would be working with others, and he worked there for a shaky fortnight before he packed it in and died.

At the next camp up the road, at Hintok, whence we sometimes drew our rations, they literally beat one man to death. He was discovered resting in the bushes down at their cutting when he ought to have been working, and the Nips took him down to the cutting in front of all the other prisoners and gave him a terrific beating up. He fainted once or twice, and was brought round by the usual Nip methods; and they continued in this way until they could bring him round no more. He wasn't quite dead yet, and was carried back to camp: but although he regained consciousness he avoided going out again on the next shift by the simple device of dying.

The Hintok Nips were on much of a par with our own Musso and The Bull: and another pretty case arose from the familiar story of the Nips demanding a working party of 120 men when the most that Hintok could muster was 105. The Nips went into the hospital tent and brought out the first fifteen of those bedded down, all of whom were dysentery cases, some of them in a very bad way indeed. They were forced to join the parade, and they set off for the cutting. One man in particular was very, very bad, but no one was allowed to lag behind and help him get along, and after several collapses he at last could go no further.

He arrived back at the camp dragging himself through the mud on his hands and knees, and was put back into the hospital: but when the Nips returned that night they knew that they'd been one short all day. They dug him out from the hospital, supported by a man on either side as he could no longer stand by himself, and then with all the typical gallantry of the Japanese, they started in and beat him up. He lay writhing on the ground whilst they beat and kicked him senseless, and although they left him breathing he was dead within two hours.

In a similar case at our own camp, three men, all very sick, passed out on the way to work, and Musso sent the squad officer back to bring them down. They were rounded up and shepherded in, and Musso, as they approached, rushed forward and started beating them with a stout bamboo. He broke the first bamboo on one of them, seized another one and broke that one too, and then got a pick handle and used it as a two-handed club. He bashed them unmercifully, and then ordered them to pick up a length of rail from the light railway, and carry it over to the rock face. It being the night shift, there was no overhead scorching sun to add to their woes; but he ordered them to hold the length of rail above their heads.

No matter how he beat them, they couldn't get it above their heads, but at last they got it to chest level, and there he kept them holding it for the best part of twenty minutes. Every time they sagged he laid in with the pick-handle, and as they couldn't even ward off the blows with their hands they were in a horrible state by the time he let them go.

That same night Musso further distinguished himself. A fellow called 'B———' (I'll just call him that lest his widow might read this) had been holding a chisel and his mate missed with his sledgehammer and crushed B———'s hand. Musso blamed B——— for not holding the chisel upright, and instead of knocking him off work and letting him have his broken fingers set, he put him onto the job of turning the big crank which worked one of the generators floodlighting the cutting. The handle was far too heavy for him to turn with his one good hand, so that he had to use the bleeding pulp of his crushed hand as well. Musso stood over him, and every time he flagged and the lights dimmed, he was beaten with a bamboo. He was kept at it for nearly an hour, during which time he twice fainted; but when he fainted for the third time he didn't come round. He was helped back to camp at the end of the shift, and he died a week later from cholera, from which he had probably already been sickening when Musso did his stuff on him.

Musso, mark you, was merely a private soldier – a private soldier under no restraint or the exercise of any control by his superiors. His was one of the few names which we managed to find out and retain – he was Superior Private Kanaga – and I must confess to having shed not a single tear when I learnt, after the war, that both he and The Bull were hanged after trial by the War Crimes Commission. What happened to Snowdrop I never learnt.

By the end of only three weeks at this new camp we were at the end of our tether. In our part of the camp alone we had fifty dead, 150 bedded down in hospital, and only fifty working; and the Australians had comparable figures but over double the size of ours.

Even the Nips realized that something had got to be done, for the men they still had were dropping of exhaustion: although they had tried to keep them going by sheer brutality alone, there comes a time when any amount of flogging seems preferable to more work.

The Nips had a bright idea. They explained that the fit working men needed more food than did those bedded down in hospital, which seemed eminently logical. The shine went off the ball, however, when they further explained that the way in which they would introduce the differential would be to keep the rations for the fit men exactly as they were, but would reduce the hospital to two meals a day.

The 'bright idea' actually had some effect. It drove a few poor devils on the brink of being hospitalized to one final effort to obtain the extra food, but it was slight as it was transitory, and never looked like stopping the rot. At last, to ameliorate the burden, the Nips introduced a programme of three eight-hour shifts a day instead of two twelve-hour shifts; but although a great relief and of assistance in finding ration parties, it had come far too late to do much good.

We now had to change shifts at midday, at 8 p.m., and at four o'clock in the morning: and those early morning parades, turning the men out at 2.30 a.m. for a meal to get them on parade at 3 a.m. to be down to the cutting by 4 a.m., were quite the worst recollections which I have of my entire captivity. The men had of necessity to be detailed overnight, but they were falling sick with such rapidity that even eight hours could make a big difference, and a man apparently fit at dinner time could well be dying by the next morning's parade time.

We would be given our quota as to how many men we had got to produce, and then we would detail this number in the evening with a few spares as well. At three o'clock the next morning our doctor and I (as the squad commander) would go along the ranks to try and pick out the worst. We could send the few worst back to the hospital and condemn the rest to the working party, but that was not the easiest of decisions, for in addition to the genuinely sick one got the inevitable occasional malingerer feigning sick to avoid the working party.

We'd get them out on parade, a huddled, muttering mob, most of them sitting down and maybe one or two who had developed cholera overnight rolling about on the ground at the back choking up the foul slimy froth that meant one thing only, whilst others would have pilchard tins containing what were known as 'rice water stools' – the opaque liquid discharge from the bowels which a cholera patient produces – as proof of their condition.

We still had to look out for shams, and one man in particular I remember. He had been caught shamming twice already, and a week later when on parade he claimed that he was now passing rice water stools. He hadn't got a specimen with him, nor had he vomited since he came on parade: and I ordered him to go off and produce a specimen for me to see. Cholera patients normally produce them every ten or fifteen minutes, and so my request was not entirely unreasonable; when he failed to appear with the necessary, I sent him off to the cutting. He did his shift, but collapsed on the journey home, and sure enough died of cholera three days later – almost certainly aggravated by working whilst already in the throes, for after all they didn't all die and nearly ten per cent recovered. It was I who had ordered him out instead of bedding him down in hospital, and so it was I who sent him to a certain death when he might have had at least a slim chance of recovery, which did my conscience no good.

It got worse. 'Whilst there is life there is hope', and one could never say that a man was *certain* to die. You could say that whereas if you sent 'A' out he would almost certainly die, but put into hospital he would have a one in ten chance of surviving and if you sent 'B' out he would only *probably* die, but put into hospital would have a fifty-fifty chance of survival.

I discussed this with the doctor, and we came to an unholy alliance. If we put the sickest man into hospital, he would have only a small chance of survival whilst the man

sent out would very probably die; whereas if we sent out
the sickest man to a certain death, there was a good
chance of survival for the less sick man. It was unfair on
the doctor to have to send a man to his death, and so it
was agreed that although it would be he who made the
original diagnosis, he would whisper it to me and it would
be I who ordered a man back to the hospital or out onto
the working party. 'It's murdering me you are', is a cry
that still rings in my ears – and the man was right. I was
condemning him to certain death when he might have
had an outside chance had I relegated him to the hospital:
but I might have saved the life of a man less sick than he
was.

That is not an easy thing to have on your conscience
even forty years later. I sent a number of men to certain
death, and it has forever since haunted me.

After only a very short while at the new camp I could no
longer go down to the cutting as a squad leader, and so I
spent my time in camp, parading parties, digging graves,
and keeping the required 'strength returns'. The strength
returns required by the Nips were easy. They contained
only three lines 'strength yesterday', 'died', and 'strength
today'. I must confess that I lied, and submitted false
returns. Our ration issue was based upon 'strength today',
and I delayed reporting deaths to get a bit of extra rice into
the camp.

My first dollop of malaria, at the old camp, had left me
with an inability to take food for several days, and that in
turn left me with beri-beri. The march up to the new camp
had done little to improve it, and I shortly went down with
a second dose of malaria and then a third, each, in the
absence of even minimal quantities of quinine, let alone
more sophisticated drugs, lasting for over a week. My
beri-beri got an increasing grip on me, and my feet and
ankles swelled up. I could no longer get my boots on, and
had to go bare foot. To complete my happiness I had also
developed a 'jungle ulcer' the size of a half-crown on my
shin and continued, with around half of the camp, to be
harried with violent diarrhoea.

The diarrhoea was not, we found, to be caused solely by
dysentery or by cholera, but by worms. We had picked up

some nasty little worms called 'Strongyloides', which in no way killed you but did your bowels no good whatsoever. They were nevertheless unwelcome, but had a ball in their chosen resort of your intestines. They kept you running over to the latrine at highly frequent intervals.

The latrine was way off in the jungle over 80 yards away, reached by a long, twisting, tortuous single-track path that wound its way through the dense bamboo and was inches deep in wet mud. By day it was unpleasant enough, particularly when it was raining, picking one's way with bare feet (beri-beri precluding the wearing of boots): but to make it worse, I seemed to hear the call of the wild even more frequently by night time than I did during the day.

On one memorable occasion I achieved the minor miracle of getting up there in time, but in coming back groping my way in the inky darkness, I strayed from the narrow path and for ten or fifteen minutes I stumbled about, getting myself more lost every moment.

My bare, swollen feet were being badly damaged on the jutting roots and the jagged rocks, although being quite numb from the beri-beri they didn't really hurt me: and I was sprawling into and savagely wrestling with springy, catapulting bamboo clumps, jabbing and scratching myself on the sword-sharp, knife-edged split stems, and having a thoroughly poor time until at last I tripped and fell into the stream.

This did not immediately improve my frayed temper, but actually it was a blessing, for I knew that the stream led down to the camp by the cook-house: and paddling gingerly along I found my sorrowful way back to the clearing and thence to my tent. I was much too exasperated to count myself lucky, but I might very well have come to more painful harm than I did, for the surrounding jungle was liberally inhabited by big black scorpions, 4 inches across at the 'arms', who resented keenly the indignity of being trodden on. They did not kill you, but their sting, so I was told (I never personally experienced one) could be very, very painful.

The latrine, to the special Nip design, was one of the

most memorable and disgusting of all of Thailand's features, all of them in that loathsome land conforming to the same style. It would consist of a long trench, 12 to 20 feet long, 18 inches wide, and 8 feet deep, with slats of bamboo placed at intervals all the way along. Between the slats were gaps 6 to 8 inches wide, and you used the slats as footrests, and crouched above the slots hovering like bombers in long, matey rows.

Having neither lids nor the labour necessary for digging sufficient trenches for our numbers – we only managed to dig one at a time by taking the sick from the hospital tents and working them in reluctant relays in half-hour stretches – within a week a trench would be full almost to the brim and become a festering breeding ground for blue-bottles and flies. A mass of big, healthy looking maggots seethed on the surface 6 inches deep. They crawled up the sides, along the slats, and all round the immediate vicinity, swarming over your feet and wriggling in and out between your toes if you were barefooted, or crawling in through the lace holes if you could still wear boots.

Many men in the urgency of the all-prevalent diarrhoea and dysentery were not too accurate in aiming at the slots, and so the slats received almost equal proportions, leading one to regret the beri-beri enforced absence of boots even more: but even so, many poor wretches, too weak to make the necessary pilgrimage up from their tents half a dozen times an hour, lay around in the nearby bushes in the sickening squalor the whole day through.

The local type of squitters gave one very little warning, and the dark nights with the twisting path had inevitable results. Every morning we turned out a party with shovels and buckets of ashes from the cook-house; but we couldn't keep pace, and even when we cleared a new dead straight path and kept a bonfire burning all night as a beacon, the time factor still beat many, and the sordid filthiness continued.

Men would creep out of their tents by night and make no effort to reach the latrine, but would make for the nearest bush or even the drainage trench around their own tent and not troubling to get a shovel. On all the paths and the surrounding bushes, and even by the cook-house and by the stream, one would stir up significant little clusters of buzzing flies, and the whole camp was little better than one gigantic sty.

The time factor wasn't everything, for conditions now were at such a level that many men had ceased to care. Living like animals, sleeping like animals, treated worse than animals, they were fast degenerating into an animal mentality. Their sense of values set completely at naught, they'd lost their remaining shreds of decency, self-respect, and self-control: their crude, primitive instincts were all that they had left.

Men simply let themselves go, those in hospital knowing that they were dying, and wearily giving up hope, making no attempt to struggle on and sullenly waiting for the end.

Apathy and callousness went hand in hand as the dominant emotions. I became quite friendly with one of the officers from Hintok later on, and he told me of one occasion when one of their men deliberately committed suicide one lunch time by jumping from the cliff top. No one so much as got up to look, let alone recover the body or to make sure that he was dead. A man could lie, and men did lie, prostrate by the roadside spewing up his very life in the filthy grey-green bubbly froth that spells cholera, and no one paused to give him a hand for fear of infection. If eventually he did get back to camp, it was well-nigh impossible to get anyone to help him with his kit over to the hospital tents, for the same reason – fear of infection. He was already as good as dead, so why take any risks?

Typical of the spirit of the times was an argument which I one day overheard myself between some men in the ration queue discussing salt. One of the things which one can do for cholera is to pump in salt water to replace dehydration and alleviate the cramps, giving it either in the form of saline drinks or directly by injection into a main vein. The Nips had refused to give us any extra salt for this purpose, and so we withdrew every grain of the salt ration from the cook-house and gave it to the doctors, leaving none to the cook-house for cooking. The man I overheard voiced the opinion 'Why should the bleeding choleras get all the salt? It just makes the food worse for us, and they're going to die anyway' – and yet salt water was the only treatment or hope of relief which we could give them, the slender thread by which a few of them might cling to life.

The cholera tents, down in the hollow at the back of the camp on the Australian side, were frightful beyond description. The blotched, stinking, emaciated victims lay packed like sardines twenty or thirty to a tent, occasionally groaning or twitching into activity and crying feebly for orderlies with bedpans, but most of them lying quite still. Bedpans, quite naturally, were merely sections of large bamboos, slit in half lengthways, and most difficult to hit in a hurry, and the over-worked sweating orderlies (who weren't trained medical orderlies at all, but merely semi-sick men detailed to the job) could no more cope with the situation than could their semi-conscious patients, and the whole place, tents and surroundings alike, was simply a disgusting and fly-ridden midden.

Huddled on the dripping chungs, stark naked or covered with sacks, bits of blanket, or rotting clothing, it was difficult to see whether some of them were alive or dead. The jaw would have dropped, the lips drawn back in a snarling hideous grin, whilst the eyes, wide open, gazed vacantly up with a fixed, sightless stare. There they would stay, quite motionless, for as much as forty-eight hours, even the eyelids having ceased to blink, still faintly breathing but otherwise alive in name only; and if their eyelids had ceased to blink, the chances were that the ants would come along and eat out their eyes before they died.

In the fierce early days of the epidemic they were not all so quiet, several going insane and others screaming and raving all through the night with the agonizing cramps – the main pain from cholera coming from severe cramps to the belly.

One man, off his head, crawled up and down his tent clubbing everyone else with the heel of his boot. He was calmed down by one of the orderlies, and appeared to go quiet; but within half an hour he was back playing the same game again, and so they took him outside and left him to die alone in the open.

Others, with the instinct of wounded animals, stole out of the tents and crept into the jungle to die in solitude, in an illusion of freedom instead of in captivity: whilst still others, with brains swinging back and forth on the borders of derangement, fought and squabbled over futile trifles with their last ebbing breaths.

Two men lay side by side for a whole day disputing possession of a groundsheet. Both were far too weak to move, both had a claw-like hand on one side of it, but neither had sufficient strength to pull it away from the other. There they lay hour after hour hurling abuse at one another, until at nightfall one died and the other got the prize, which he kept for two whole hours before he died in turn.

I was in constant touch with the goings-on in the cholera tents since as part of my job of filling in the strength returns I had to visit every tent each day to find out how many men had died. I did the cholera tents first, and then the dysentery tents, since those were where virtually all of the deaths were occuring, and I could send up advance warning to the cremation party as to with how many corpses they would have to cope that afternoon. More about the cremation party later.

Just above the cholera tents, and above the lime pit, we had a 'post-cholera' tent for those few who had apparently got over it, and some dysentery tents, growing in size daily, but not yet at their peak. Whereas the cholera claimed its victims in the first four weeks and then petered out, dysentery took longer, and most of the deaths took place in our last two to three weeks at the camp, or even afterwards at our next camp.

Yet further up the hill we had the beri-beri and malaria tents, which were not so smelly: we also had a special tent set aside for the growing number of men with bad cases of tropical ulcers. These ulcers were found in every camp along the line in Thailand, although they had never troubled us down in Malaya; and for sheer nagging pain they took a great deal of beating.

They usually started with a little pin prick or a scratch on the leg from a bamboo shoot whilst one was marching down to the cutting, but rapidly developed into huge open sores with a raised-up rim, the centre hollowed out like the crater of a volcano, usually about half an inch deep although often deeper, reaching and exposing the bone having eaten away all the intervening flesh.

Within a week they would spread to the diameter of a jam jar lid, about 3 inches across being the most fashionable size. The popular place was the leg, mostly on the shin or on the calf, although kneecaps and ankle joints were particularly painful, hurting every time one flexed. Several men had them on the toes or arms, and one had one all over his cheek and eyelid (he lost his eye rather painfully before he got gangrene and died); but the legs were by far the most usual location, and most people had several ulcers at a time rather than just one.

With no drugs, dressings, or anti-septics (anti-biotics didn't then exist), there was little that the doctors could do, and the treatment consisted simply of scraping out the pus with an egg spoon, bathing with warm salt water, and putting one's trust in Providence.

Scraps of shirt tail, bits of sarong, and strips of banana leaf were made to serve as dressings, but they were hopelessly inadequate and couldn't even keep off the flies. We'd sit in a row by the doctor's tent each evening waiting for our turn to come to be scraped, with the blue-bottles from the big latrine, attracted by the smell, swarming around the succulent putrefaction; and scores of men had the additional trouble of getting their ulcers full of maggots.

The orderlies worked two at a time, the first with a pair of tweezers picking out the maggots, whilst the second followed up with the egg spoon and the salt water: to hear the cries and stifled sobs of each man as the spoon scraped home was not very soothing to the nerves of the others still waiting in the queue.

Some people will tell you that maggots in a wound are a good thing, and are Nature's way of keeping it clean: but some people will believe anything. Maggots, or at least *our* brand of maggots, made the wound itch even more. So far from keeping it clear of pus, they positively revelled in it, and as they gambolled about and disturbed quiescent spots, they were nothing but a nuisance – and we didn't much care for the idea of where they'd bred and come from anyway.

The awful nagging pain of a large ulcer put sleep right out of the question – for of course we had no morphia or other opiates to deaden or relieve the pain – and quite a few of those who died nominally from ulcers did so as much from the sheer exhaustion of a week's wakefulness as from the general toxaemia.

You didn't die from one ulcer, but sometimes you would have several and they would get out of hand and would join up to form one huge infection. David Eastham, whom I have mentioned earlier, was an example. He had one stretching from his knee to his ankle, the whole of the flesh from his shin had disappeared, and he had a strip of flesh that had once been his calf still attached top and bottom, but you could see his shin bone and then see daylight between the back of that bone and his 'calf'. Usually, at that stage, it meant an amputation of the leg; but David resisted, kept his leg, and miraculously survived, being a man of exceptionally strong character.

Not all such aggravated cases survived. An ulcer tent could be told long before one entered it from the stench of putrefying flesh; and in another camp from ours, a large one with 1,600 men, there were over fifty amputations. They had only one saw in the camp, used on the wood dump all day sawing wood for the cook-house and the cremation fires: but on request the saw would be sterilized by the cook-house in boiling water, handed over to the doctor for him to chop the fellow's leg off, and then returned to the waiting wood party. Gangrene was common rather than uncommon, and it is scarcely surprising that out of those fifty odd amputations, only one solitary man lived to return to Malaya.

In our camp we were very lucky. Amongst the Australians there was a man who was reckoned to be amongst the finest surgeons in Australia. Instead of waiting for the ulcers to spread, he used to cut them clean out when still only a few inches across, leaving a great round patch as clean as raw fillet steak; and although some of them turned septic again (as did David

Eastham's) and their owner either lost his leg or died, the large majority healed up and Kevin (the Australian surgeon, whose surname I cannot remember) undoubtedly saved a great number of highly dangerous amputations.

He had with him a small case of surgical instruments which he'd carried in his pack, but he was no man to be daunted by lack of fine equipment. In a case of pleurisy, when he needed to drain some fluid from a lung, he sharpened up a bamboo twig (bamboos being hollow down the inside) as he hadn't got the proper tools, and with that he pierced the lung and personally sucked out the juice.

Bamboo had many peculiar uses, another medical adaption being that of using it in lieu of a large hypodermic needle. To pump salt water into a cholera patient you need a syringe as big as a grease gun, and there being nothing of the sort available, the job was done with a bamboo 'needle', the water being fed in by gravity from a paper funnel down through the rubber tubing from a stethoscope.

With increasingly blunt axes and saws, and no such thing as a plane, we couldn't use the plentiful supplies of hardwoods such as teak or ironwood to make such items as we required, and so bamboo, being soft and easily worked, had to serve for everything.

We lay on bamboo chungs in tents with bamboo poles and bamboo pickets, while bamboo scaffolding held our cooking pots above a roaring bamboo fire; we strung the pots on bamboo poles and walked along bamboo causeways to serve the rice from bamboo scoops and stuff it into our bamboo dinner pails. We stored water in big bamboos, we aired our bedding on bamboo clothes lines, bamboo bedpans were used in the sick wards, and bamboo slats held our swaying bulks above the bamboo-revetted latrines. The Nips beat us with bamboos, we made bamboo tables and stools, bamboo fences, bamboo bridges, bamboo walking sticks and bamboo crutches – big ones, little ones, green ones, yellow ones, short ones, fat ones, thin ones, thick ones, bamboos bamboos bamboos *ad nauseam*, the nauseating symbol of a nauseating land.

We built bamboo stretchers, and each day a grim little procession trudged up to the cemetery we had built further off in the jungle. We had started by cremating the corpses, but after four weeks of this the Nip guards said that they couldn't bear the smell, and that in future we should have to bury our dead. Our interpreter pointed out that with the cholera and dysentery victims, it was far safer to burn rather than bury them, but to no avail. The Imperial nostrils had been offended, and that was of primary importance. From week five onwards we buried the dead.

We had never had the resources to permit the luxury of a separate funeral pyre for each individual – we built one big fire and popped the day's whole quota of corpses onto it all together, piling some wet bamboo on once they had been burnt to keep the embers smouldering until the next day to save lighting a new fire from scratch. Even so, we had to be careful that the corpses themselves did not douse the fire.

Beri-beri was the trouble here. It involves tremendous dropsy, not just in the feet and ankles but in the more serious cases also in the stomach, the face, and the testicles. It is surprising just how much fluid a body can contain in those circumstances. Unless one was careful, a body on the fire could burst, dampening down the fire and probably spraying scalding water over anyone standing near: we soon learnt that a serious beri-beri case should be speared and left to drain before the body was put on the fire.

The cremation party, like everyone else, became completely callous. With death as your familiar, a corpse lost all of its traditional majesty, and so far from being an object of hushed reverence, it became nothing but a smelly damned nuisance.

Sometimes it even became a grotesque butt for humour, as instanced when the muscles of a burning body contracted and it sat up. Flesh still covered the rib cage, but that made it act like a chimney, and smoke and licks of flame were emerging from the burnt out eye sockets and the mouth. 'Oi! Look at old Bert!' remarked one of the stokers. 'Thinks 'e's a fuckin' dragon!'; and then, with delighted chuckles the little group fell to discussing what a grand chap their old pal Bert had once been.

We burnt the bodies in the afternoon, which gave the cremation party the opportunity to boil up their midday dixie of water on the fire before it was truly stoked up, and some men would put on some bamboo shoots or wild sweet potatoes to roast in the embers. If, on trying to recover them, you got the odd toe or wrist by mistake, you just threw it back and went on scrabbling for your potato, probably using a charred rib as a rake. Death had long since lost its dignity.

By the end of the fourth week, the death toll was reducing. The cholera wave was now on the wane, and so deaths were reduced from the peak of up to a dozen a day to a mere six to eight. However, the switch from burning to burying did not ease the burden. Instead of the morning being spent cutting bamboo for the fire, there was now a pit to dig, and the ground was not soft below the muddy topsoil. The Nips would not allow us any more men for the digging, and so it still had to be done by the semi-fit. My beri-beri had gone down, so that I could now get my boots on, and as I still had to prepare the strength returns and attend the parades to decide, on the doctor's recommendation, who should go down to the cutting as 'fit' and who should be returned to his tent, I was not sent down to the cutting myself, but joined the grave diggers.

As with the cremations, we could not give every man a separate grave any more than we had given the earlier casualties separate funeral pyres. We just dug one big pit for the day's quota, and tipped them all in together.

The early practice of tying the bodies up in groundsheets or blankets was reluctantly given up owing to the acute shortage of these and indeed of all wearing apparel. In fact, we had a very sticky little passage with the Nips when they learnt that earlier, a number of blankets had been burnt with the cholera corpses – blankets not only probably infected with the disease, but heavily fouled as the blanket of a cholera patient is apt to be when he loses all control over his bowels before the end. They winded up, laughably enough (in retrospect, but not then) by saying that they would deduct the value of the blankets from our pay – but as they had not issued us with any pay whatsoever since that one 'eight day week' burst at Kamburi, this threat lost much of its edge.

Nevertheless, we had to abandon the practice of burying the corpses in groundsheets or blankets, and we would just tip them in, stark naked, that day's quota all together in a tangled mass of grotesquely distorted limbs, torsos, and skull-like death's heads grinning sightlessly up at you as you shovelled on the earth.

We'd cover them up quickly to keep down the flies and the stench, and if there had not been too many and we had dug the pit deeply enough, there might even be room for another layer tomorrow: but having sealed this lot in we would breathe a sigh of relief, and I would read the short burial service over them – they all got a pukka Christian burial, no matter what their unknown religion – and on top of each communal grave we even erected a little bamboo cross.

The first phase of life in this camp, with the initial twelve-hour shifts, the tumbling figures of those available for work, and the main wave of the cholera, lasted – although it seemed for an age – only for four weeks. The change from twelve to eight hour shifts relieved the load of the individual, but it came too late to do much good, and the second phase which followed was little better than the first. The hours were shorter, but the pressure during those hours grew even worse, and the perpetual beatings, the continuing lack of food, and those ghastly night-time parades, brought us to our lowest ebb of degradation and misery.

Cowed and hopeless, we settled down from the hectic early struggle to a dull, bemused despair. The filth and squalor was gaining the upper hand, and we stumbled blindly on and on in an apathetic daze, scarcely now caring what happened next or whether we lived or died – to many, death seemed to be but a merciful release.

Although the cholera was waning, and no new cases were arising, dysentery, malaria and beri-beri which for some while had been filling the hospital, now began to fill the graveyard as well. Ulcers were coming increasingly to the fore in crippling the workforce, and the constant wet conditions and the lack of boots produced a crop of really bad trench feet, the skin rotting and peeling in patches and leaving the feet bleeding, inflamed, and raw, and an easy prey to septic poisoning.

The monsoon was still in progress, the mud in the camp was getting deeper and deeper, and it got so bad that once again we had to make use of the sick from the hospital to build little bamboo causeways everywhere, not merely to the latrine but to the cook-house and between all of the tents. At night, with the clouds covering the moon, one regularly squelched off the causeways into the glutinous mud; but although the feeling of it oozing in over your boots (if you were lucky enough to have boots) was not pleasant in itself, the rub lay not so much in the depth as in the slipperiness. If you fell over, even if you saved yourself by your hands and knees, the wet mud clung, and the river, because of the cholera, being out of bounds even for washing (one couldn't risk infection of one's towel, which would later touch one's lips) you had to try and remove the mud in what little boiled water was available – usually just a mess-tinful.

That lack of washing was in itself most demoralizing. We had no soap or toothpaste, and I had even lost my toothbrush on an evil night when the chung collapsed and dropped us all in the mud; although I personally managed to get a splash most days, many of the men went for weeks on end without attempting to clean themselves up. Long, straggly beards contrasted strangely with our shaven heads – one man had a pair of clippers and most of us had clean shaven heads as these were less itchy and less prone to lice in the sweaty conditions – but our unkempt appearance fell in well with the foul state of our unwashed clothes.

The mud was only marginally less thick inside the tents than it was outside, and all that one owned was always clammy, moist, and growing fungus. Normally, one sleeps in a tent with the head towards the outside and the feet towards the middle: but our tents leaked so badly that we slept with our heads towards the middle, and little hoops of bamboo with a groundsheet over them (like small dog kennels) covered our feet to allow the drips and the steady streams from the more open rents in the tent canvas to pour off the sides.

Figures continued to dwindle, until by the end of another three weeks it was hard for us to scrape up twenty men for each working party: but a glimmer of light appeared at the end of the tunnel. The Nips had brought up a band of native coolies, put them in a separate camp a few hundred yards away from us, and they were brought into the now nearly finished cutting to work side by side with us.

These poor unhappy coolies, mostly Tamils and Chinese, had been brought up to Thailand from Malaya, and fared even worse than we did. The bait which they had been offered was two dollars a day, four times what they had been earning in Malaya, with the threat that if they didn't 'volunteer' there would be no ration cards for their families. They had been given three months' pay in advance, which they had blithely spent on the journey up, and now they were nicely trapped, without a cent in their pockets and many hundreds of miles from home.

They were herded into camps patrolled by armed Nip guards, they were fed simply on rice and jungle stew, and then found that the Nips had the sauce to deduct half of their future pay as the 'cost of board and lodging', adding another three months' debt before they received another penny. They worked for shorter shifts than we did, and received less beating up (at first): but whereas we had doctors, even without equipment or drugs, they had no medical men or supplies whatsoever, and they were already dying off like flies in the autumn.

To us, their presence meant that we were no longer the sole source of labour, and even the Nips had realized that, as a labour force, we were about played out. The cutting was nearly finished, and hope began to arise in our breasts that with all these coolies (there were masses of them) the Nips would not consider it worthwhile to move us further up the line. They might move the 'fit', but even these were now so feeble that they couldn't last for another month, and they were also so few that we needed all of their labour to draw our rations and to run our own camp.

Our only hope of true salvation, of evacuation back to a

base in the plains, had long faded from our thoughts; resignation to the prospect of being left to rot and perish in the jungle being general. One in four was dead already, half of those who were left were not far off death, and all we craved – the best for which we craved – was some easing of the pressure so that we could die in comparative peace.

Then, at the very blackest hour, when apathy and blank despair had all but quenched our flickering spirits, orders arrived which seemed too good to be true.

The Nips had decided to write us off. Work in this sector was nearing an end anyway, and the whole of what remained of H Force was to go back to Kamburi. Not only the sick, but everyone, the fit as well, were to be withdrawn, and we were to stand by as from the next day to move in train-loads of a hundred men a day. Work meanwhile would consist only of tidying up, such as capping off latrines, and, most incredible of all, to keep us going they were sending up a meat ration, on hoof.

13   Meat

To the confusion of the sceptics, the day after we got the new orders the meat actually did arrive: a herd of fifteen bullocks. Little, scraggy, Eastern bullocks, no bigger than Dartmoor ponies, as starving as we and with their ribs all showing; but bullocks they were nonetheless, and we were told that we could slaughter one a day.

Standing by at one day's notice to move, we weren't going to risk leaving any behind, and so we decided to slaughter two a day, which proved a wise decision.

Each day from then on, little convoys of these bullocks – 'yaks' as they were popularly known amongst the troops – came plodding past our camp on their way up-country either to other prison camps or for the Nips themselves. The road was bounded by open jungle, it twisted and turned at frequent intervals, and the herds would straggle out in twos and threes over a quarter of a mile or so, so that although there was one Nip leading at the front and another at the back, there would come a time when the animals in the middle could be seen by neither. After five days of eating two a day of our original fifteen, we still had eighteen. Two yaks don't go very far amongst several hundred men, but they added enormously to the flavour of the jungle stew, and they did even more for our morale.

The other promise of the letter, evacuation to the plains, was not fulfilled so speedily, and four more weary weeks (by the end of which we had run out of yaks) crawled by. We were not immediately relieved from sending men down to the cutting, but they cut out the night shift and ration parties became an alternative for the semi-sick instead of an additional task for the off-duty men, and although the death roll was still mounting, convalescents were no longer forced out on parade. Within a fortnight, the rails were laid on the sleepers, and working parties stopped.

The jetty, from where we drew our rations, had a little Thai hut selling eggs, bananas, tinned pilchards, and peanuts (rich in vitamin B). Up until now, the stouter souls amongst the ration parties had taken a pack or a haversack and would bring back a few private supplies in addition to their sacks of rice: but it was only a tiny dribble and was snapped up by anyone who still had any money. For the hospital, we had managed to scrape up a small party of five or six men once a week – a couple from the cook-house, the Australian Padre, one MO and perhaps two other officers – who would bring in milk powder and eggs: but we had to do it very surreptitiously, for had we done it too often or sent bigger parties, the Nip reaction would have been obvious – more men available for the cutting – and so we had to keep it down although our need for the stuff was clearly desperate.

Once the rails were laid and the working parties stopped, there were no such constraints, and we could send down a carrying party each day: but by the cussedness of fate supplies were becoming scarcer, and demand began to exceed supply. With the river in full spate, fewer and fewer 'freelance' barges troubled to come right up, having sold their wares further downstream, and those that did get as far as us were very soon sold out.

As prisoners, we could still only go down to the jetty in a body with a Nip guard in charge, whilst the new swarms of coolies, although nominally under guard, found it easier to slip off through the jungle, and could well clear a barge before we even got there. The supplies were fewer, but there were many extra customers, and if we could collect two hundred eggs, some dried milk, and a couple of basketsful of peanuts, we did not count it as a bad outing.

A less desirable aspect of 'Smokey Joe's', as we had christened the Thai hut on the jetty, was the roaring trade which they did in 'saki', the crude fiery spirit made from rice and beloved by the Nips. Our camp guard consisted only of one Lance-Corporal and six private soldiers, and they would go off en masse on jolly boozing parties (to be fair to them, they hadn't had any booze for months on end either), leaving only one of the privates to 'guard' the whole camp; and when they all returned fighting drunk, it was not always pleasant for the prisoners.

One, the little Nip Quartermaster who was in charge of the tool shed, had been ordered back down country, and whilst he was waiting he had a long drawn solo bout, sleeping all day and getting drunker every night for over a week, as he went down to Smokey Joe's with his pals. His special choice of venue on his return would be the cook-house, where he could see what he was doing as it would be after dark but there would be a fire burning, and there he would rampage about knocking down the cooks and hitting everyone in sight before reeling off into the hospital lines terrorizing the patients.

On the fifth night he lurched into the tent I was in. I myself was huddled under a blanket having a malaria rigor, and he took no notice of me; but the man next to me, by the name of Pilkington, had a sorry time, being beaten about the head and then pulled off the chung by his moustache down into the aisle. This, to a British Captain from a little rat of a drunken Nip private: and there was nothing whatsoever that we could do to prevent or to avenge this or a hundred other similar humiliations. On the following night he grabbed the cook-house's one and only butcher's knife (which had been in use on the Yaks), and as he started on his rounds we managed to get the rest of the Nip Guard to suppress him (which they did none too gently), and to our great relief he was sent off back to Tarso the next morning.

Three weeks had stolen by since we had been told that we were to be evacuated; and then new orders came in which were scarcely what we had been hoping for. Our seventy fittest men would not be evacuated, but would march on that night. The Australians were to produce fifty, whereas our smaller sub-camp had only to produce twenty: but even so to make up twenty we had to include several hospital cases who looked to be on the mend and probably ready for discharge fairly soon anyway.

Off they went with their usual Christmas trees of packs, haversacks, rolled up blankets and whatever, and I for one did not expect to see many of them again. By the grace of God I was wrong, and they had very few further deaths. For the record, however, out of the 253 men who came up from our first working camp to the second, only 89 eventually survived, with 164 dying. They weren't all dead yet, but as the death roll was still rising, if the evacuation orders didn't come soon, there wouldn't be many left to evacuate.

They *did* come soon. Only shortly after the new working party had left, there was the usual frantic rush and we were told that we should start moving the next day, split into four train-loads at one train a day. Monty was to be the Camp Quartermaster at the new base camp, and so off he went with the first train-load (otherwise consisting solely of Australians), while I was left in charge of the non-Australian camp, which was allocated train 3.

We built two dozen bamboo stretchers for carrying the sickest men, and made a large stock of clean bedpans – for although many men were far too sick to be moved, with the camp about to be closed down completely, we couldn't leave anyone behind, and even the dying had got to go with us. The Nips, nothing if not realists, had recognized this at the initial briefing of Train Commanders, and had said that each party should carry two shovels so that we could bury our dead *en route*; two to save time having two men digging each grave rather than unnecessarily delaying the party. They said 'to bury our dead', not 'to bury any man who *might* die', because they knew as well as we did that deaths *en route* were inevitable.

Trains 1 and 2 went off, but on the very eve of the departure of my train, number 3, I was told that there had been another change of plan. Originally we had been told to produce train-loads of one hundred, but that left an odd number at the end. I was having the luxury of a final wash in half a kerosene tinful of water when I was summoned to the Nip Guard tent. Wrapping my towel around my middle I went in, to be told that the 'odd men' instead of going on train 5 on their own, would now be split between trains 3 and 4.

That sounded sensible enough, but it was now 9 p.m. and

it meant that just over twenty men who had not expected to move for two days more, now had to get ready to move by 5 a.m., in eight hours' time. I conferred with my senior NCO and with the doctor, and we selected the names of the men who were to go; the NCO went off to warn those affected, whilst I was left to wrestle with the bumph.

The Nips had demanded detailed nominal rolls, in alphabetical order, giving not only names but names of next of kin, dates of birth, civil occupations, diseases from which currently suffering, and a large medical history sheet covering the period since coming up to Thailand. These had been prepared by our Adjutant three days earlier, when we first got the movement order: and as he himself was a member of my train party number 3 it would normally have been he who had to produce the revised rolls rather than me. However, he had chosen that evening of all evenings to go into a malaria rigor, which was why I had to cope with the revisions. He'd had three bouts of malaria in ten weeks, and was in the middle of one now; to improve the shining hour he had gone delirious and kept crawling out from under his blanket and sitting stark naked and gibbering on the end of the chung. We kept putting him back under his blanket as the night was pretty chilly, but he continued to bounce out and as the helpful Adjutant in the moment of crisis, he wasn't a great success. Fortunately he got over it by midnight, and was able to accompany us at five.

Meanwhile, I had to revise his nominal rolls, which I did by the light of one candle thoughtfully provided by the Nips along with the necessary supplies of paper. I got them finished by 11 p.m., and was able to get some sleep: then at 5 a.m. we started to get all of the men on parade, stretcher parties detailed to stretchers, a breakfast of rice served and 'packed rations' of rice issued. By 6 a.m. our sorry little convoy set off for the last time down the old familiar track to the cutting, for this was not the sort of railway which went in for formal stations, and it was just as easy to stop the train at our cutting than it was anywhere else.

I was one short on my quota of men, which caused initial trouble with the Nips when counting us until I convinced them that one man had died during the night and that I had not had time to re-do the nominal rolls. We had seventeen men on stretchers, which meant we needed sixty-eight stretcher bearers, as we had not sufficient men fit enough to do 'two to a stretcher', so we had to make it four, one to each corner. These men had not only to carry the stretchers but also their own kits and the kits of the stretcher cases: obviously we did not make very fast progress. The slippery pathway had not improved after ten weeks of use.

The people detailed for train 4 the next day came along and gave us some help, but even so we had considerable difficulty. Two of the stretchers broke – they were only lashed together with jungle creeper – dropping the patients heavily on the ground: one of these died the following day, although we had at least got him to the train. He had the distinction of being the first man to require the use of our shovels.

To qualify for the luxury of a stretcher one had to be very ill indeed, literally not able to walk a step; and there were many doomed to go on foot who were not really much better off. They could do perhaps 100 yards in one go, have a short rest, and then totter on for another 100: it made me very glad indeed when, on counting them, I confirmed that they were all down in the cutting by the time that the train arrived.

It wasn't much of a train – a small diesel engine with two open trucks – but at least it was pointing in the right direction back down country. The stretchers took up most of the floor space, leaving all the rest of the men standing up around the edges, sitting on the sides, standing on the buffers or clinging onto the engine, whilst I myself occupied the place of honour sitting on the engine's headlight.

It wasn't for very long. It carried us down for only 4 miles to Tempie, which was the new steam railhead. Tempie was about half way between our old first working camp and our second, the track up to there from Tarso now being completed and tested. The further stretch, up to our second working camp was still being tested and run in, which was why it was still being used only by the little light Diesels, the Nips not yet risking using it for the heavier and more valuable steam engines.

When we got there, we were ordered to get all of our stretchers and kit and carry them down to the far end of the sidings to wait for the steam train; and after waiting for several hours, we saw the train come in. It went right up to the far end at which we had arrived, and in a frantic hurry we had to tote all our stuff back again and get aboard.

Although the next section of the line was now officially finished and open, it did not compare for smoothness with British Rail. We went at the most at about fifteen miles an hour, but we bumped and lurched and cavorted about like mad things, and twice we passed upturned trucks at the bottom of ravines. In the early afternoon we sweltered breathlessly in the broiling sun, until the heavens opened and we shivered in a tropical downpour: although none of our sick actually died on this stretch of the journey, several weren't far off dying, and it wasn't exactly a picnic.

Dysentery harries its victims frequently, and with a fair quota aboard our medical orderlies did yeoman service. Two men, stretcher cases, both of whom were to die before the next day was out, were already too feeble either to call for or to cope with bedpans: the narrowness of the split bamboo bedpans themselves was made additionally apparent for everyone by the bumping and rocking of the trucks and the effect of all this, combined with the stench of scores of running jungle ulcers, left a vivid imprint of that journey on the mind of every one of us.

From Tempie we went non-stop to Tarso, and there we were told that we should be stopping for the night. We'd had a taste of Tarso on the way up, when the Nip Guards didn't know the way from the railway sidings to the transit camp, and so this time I decided that we would leave all our stretcher cases at the sidings, get all our fit men and our kits to the camp first of all, and come back for the stretchers later.

It was as well that we did, for this time our solitary Guard didn't know the way either. Eventually we reached the well remembered Nip Guard hut; our man got directions and this time led us off to a proper hutted transit hospital of four long earth-floor attap huts with a cook-house, and two British MOs in charge.

The MOs were very good to us, and having their own tame Nip interpreter were actually able to get a lorry to bring up the stretcher cases. They had, however, no labour force to call upon, and so we had to get our own meal ready, from cutting some bamboo for the fire to peeling the pumpkins and cooking the stew.

We had expected to be moved on again at dawn the next day, but just before we got to bed we were told that the Nips had decided to leave us for twenty-four hours. I passed the news along, and the next morning we all lay long and luxuriously abed. We rested to our fill, and then we had to get the fitter men down to a little work.

There was a store of food in the cook-house, but we had to gather our own firewood, cook, mend the stretchers which had broken their lashings and strengthen up the rest; there was one man to get buried, and I sent a small party off to the river to buy eggs and bananas. After lunch I personally retired from the fray to have yet another malaria rigor, but fortunately it was a very short one and I was up and doing again by tea time.

The Nips had told us that we would be moved on at dawn the next day, and that if we put the stretcher cases out by the entrance, they would take them down to the sidings by lorry. We should have to take them all, and could not leave any here, as this was strictly a transit camp with no permanent facilities (which was why it was empty when we arrived).

At 6 o'clock in the evening they changed their minds, and said that the stretcher cases were not to move after all but would stay here in Tarso. I knew too well what this would mean, and the patients knew it too – they were to be left to die with no one to look after them, which didn't tend to cheer them up. We'd buried the one I mentioned in the morning, a second had died in the afternoon, and two more were already in a coma. That left thirteen out of the seventeen who had started the journey with us, and although none of them had stood the trip well, they all without exception preferred to risk the further trip to the prospect of staying here at Tarso.

Soon after it was dark the Nips again changed the orders. The stretcher cases would go with us after all, and so when we eventually paraded in the morning, they were all brought out. Not all, actually, for there were now only twelve: two had died the previous day, the two in a coma were still unconscious, and another one had started choking blood during the night, and so those three we did leave.

The twelve were put by the entrance, and the rest of us marched off – 'marched' being scarcely a fair description, for of course we could make no attempt at keeping ranks or files or keeping in step: and we just ambled along as best we would. Twos and threes slunk along, broken shambling wrecks of what had once been men, little groups kept resting by the roadside, and although it was only a mile to the sidings, by the time we got there the column stretched for a good half of the distance.

When all of us were there (my senior NCO had been bringing up the rear) the Nips ordered us into the wagons – covered box-cars this time instead of the previous open ballast trucks – and my NCO and I counted each box-carful in. We were one man short.

We counted again, and were still one short, and the Nips began to get angry. I still had the nominal rolls, and so I stood back on a pile of sleepers and called out the names. As the men were all inside the box-cars, hearing was not easy, but I got about three quarters of the way through before I got no reply at all and my worst forebodings were confirmed. The missing man was one who had given trouble already, claiming that he couldn't walk although the doctors had said that he was no worse than anyone else, and I'd had to have him chased out of the hut to get him on parade at all before leaving camp.

I'd seen the whole column, including him, out through the camp entrance, but evidently he'd fallen out *en route* for a rest by the roadside, hidden himself in the bushes and thus given the slip to my NCO, and made his way back to the camp in the hope of getting on a stretcher.

By now the Nips were really cross, and I was told in a somewhat blunt manner that I was no good. They slapped my face, slapped my Sergeant's face, and turned back to me and knocked me over. The stomach kicking had just started when the engine gave a timely whistle and immediately began to chug out. Leaving the Nips to gather up the medical history sheets which I had dropped, I made for the moving train where helping hands hauled me aboard, and off I went with a muttered hymn of thanks to the driver.

The lorry with the stretchers never arrived, of course, and so our twelve men were left to their fate. I learnt later from one of the Tarso doctors, who eventually joined us at the base camp, that seven of them died within a fortnight, although five of them survived. What happened to my 'missing man' I never learnt.

It was quite a pleasant journey once we had got through these preliminaries, for we'd plenty of room not being cluttered up with stretchers: and shortly after leaving we stopped at Wam-Po, which had once been a railhead before Tarso had been created. It was now virtually deserted, but there was a little Thai hut selling food, which greatly brightened our two-hour halt.

We got hot sweet coffee, bananas, hard boiled eggs, and sago cakes. Hanging up by the side of the hut were four ready roasted chickens. For these the Thai was demanding six ticals each, which was far more than anyone could or would pay; but they were hanging perilously within reach of the milling crowd of would-be buyers, and, shocking to relate, somehow the bamboo pole on which they were hanging got broken, and in the resulting confusion all four disappeared.

Never in my life, either before or since, have I enjoyed a wing of chicken more than I did that day, after it had been properly sterilized on a shovel in a jet of boiling water from the engine; and even the fact that the self same shovel had been used for grave digging a day earlier had no effect upon anybody's appetite. With that and a bunch of bananas I was still feeling pretty happy when, after travelling all afternoon, we reached Kamburi and entered at long last our promised 'land of rest'.

14   Heaven

Our first reaction to the sight of the new camp was one of wonderment and almost of disbelief. It was a palace.

When we had come through Kamburi on the way up, we had had a stretch of scrub alongside the road between two small kampongs, the only building being that used as a cook-house and all of us sleeping under bushes or in the open.

Now, a little further back along the line, there was a huge camp of proper attap huts. We were ordered off the train, over a fragile-looking bridge over the river, and then into the camp, which even had a fence around it so that we had to go through a proper gate.

The camp was not yet fully built, but the Nips had a gang of Thai coolies (not British prisoners) still erecting new huts at one end. There was a broad road down the middle, and a row of huts end-on to the road at either side sticking out like the ribs on a herring-bone. We were led into an empty hut, which even had chungs already in place; we sorted ourselves out, putting all of the dysentery cases down at the far end where they were nearer the ready-dug latrine at the back. Even the latrine had an attap roof. Buckingham Palace had nothing on this!

We were soon greeted by the H Force Commander, who was already there with his meagre staff, and by Monty who had been on train 1; they filled us in on the general situation.

There were about 2,000 prisoners here, mostly H Force but with numerous others; there were no working parties and all that we had to do was to look after ourselves. Even the rations came in by lorry, as did firewood. Water was a problem, but that was another story. Roughly across the middle of the camp was a fence separating the huts at the far end of the road, which was a camp for native coolies. Our end of the camp had not got a canteen, but the coolie camp had: and although it was officially forbidden, it was easy enough to buy things through the fence, which consisted only of 4-foot high bamboo stakes about 3 feet apart, with three thin bamboo horizontals.

The perimeter fence was of similar construction, and merely marked the boundary rather than present any obstacle; but whereas we ourselves were not allowed outside, neither were the Thais from the neighbouring kampongs allowed inside. Although again officially forbidden, this is no way inhibited a roaring trade with the locals through the fence, and so food supplementing was easy.

As we had entered the camp from the railway, each man had been allowed in singly, having been sprayed with disinfectant by a Nip orderly with a stirrup pump; and this terrific display of modern hygiene seemed to us to be the symbol of our return to civilization. Our clothes soon dried off, and we had scarcely got ourselves into our hut when we were served with a hot meal prepared by our co-prisoners who were already there – we didn't even have to cook it for ourselves. There was rice and a stew which tasted very much better than the up-jungle stew of radish tops, and which we found to include pumpkins, bean sprouts, yams, onions, and even tiny little shreds of pork. Neither the Ritz nor the Dorchester could have done us any better.

For three weeks we remained in that hut, a heavenly three weeks compared with the previous three months, whilst the few remaining huts were completed and the balance of H Force trickled in. We had quite a few men die, but the rest of us were definitely getting stronger.

We had roll calls night and morning, but even the Nips realized that this was meant to be a hospital, and so instead of having all of us out of the huts on parade, they came round and counted us on the chungs. In actual fact, the Nip would usually just stand by the hut entrance and order us to 'number off', which we did in English so he couldn't understand anyway. At the end he would ask 'O.K.?' and I would interpret the total into Japanese. He would collect my little slip and then he would trot off none the wiser. My own bed space was nearest the entrance, and as Hut Commander it was my job to have prepared the usual simple little Nip three-line strength return of 'strength yesterday', 'died', and 'strength today', the last figure being used for the ration issue.

Whilst the huts were being completed and parties had been trickling in, we had simply been put into huts on a train-load by train-load basis; but once they were all up it was decided to have a grand reorganization, with everyone reshuffled into wards that went by disease instead of by party, the five groups being: dysentery, ulcers, beri-beri, malaria, and 'others'. There were not very many 'others', as the vast majority of us qualified under at least one if not two or three of the other main categories. The cholera epidemic had virtually finished, and those who had had it were very largely already dead: whilst the few survivors were merely a minority amongst the 'others' category.

It was chaos.

There were no empty huts to act as 'reservoirs', and the difficulty was to move new men in until the existing occupants had been moved out. We had no proper quota of trained medical orderlies, although each train party had detailed a number of its own men for this unpleasant job whilst we were in our 'party huts'; a substantial number of these now took the opportunity of the move to desist from these duties and move themselves to designated 'disease' huts. Men lay for hours in the open, abandoned by their 'orderlies', and a number went two whole days without a meal, for the food distribution just collapsed and few men who could grab a second meal in the confusion worried at the thought that some other man would inevitably lose his.

Many men were quite unfit to be moved anyway, for scores throughout the camp were on their last legs: in the four or five days starting with the change-round the death rate shot up like a rocket. Ward 14, the new main dysentery ward, suffered most, where in three days there were fifteen deaths from a total hut strength of eighty-five. It tailed off rapidly after this, for all of the next fortnight's 'probables' had been killed off: all the same Ward 14 lost fifty over the next two months, and a nasty dirty smelly death it is too.

New 'orderlies' were detailed, but not all of them turned up, and the work in the wards was largely left undone, although prostrate dysentery patients require a great deal of attention. Many could not wait whilst an orderly fetched a bed pan, fouling their beds and their blankets in quarter-hourly spasms, and many others, still capable of a greater measure of self-control, were yet so feeble that they had to be lifted and held in position. The entire chung was running with filth, with the men themselves, too weak to move, lying in the muck tormented by blue-bottles and maggots and lice.

Things were only kept going by the few fitter patients and those orderlies who did turn up; they, in despair of keeping the worst cases cleaned, moved them all down to the far end of the hut, steeling themselves against the pathetic and terrified pleading and even sobbing of men who, taking one look at the company they were joining, knew that they were being put down there to die.

Only by such measures was there any hope of saving the remainder: virtually abandoning those more obviously doomed to die, with all efforts concentrated on the others. Men who for six or more weeks had not had a drop of water to their bodies were given the luxury of a wash, their blankets were washed and dried for them, and a reasonable service of bedpans was maintained, so that gradually one end of the hut was cleaned up and kept clean; although the other still ran like a sewer, a pestilential fly-ridden death-haunted midden.

I was extremely lucky. Before the war I had been in training to become a chartered accountant, and although the war had broken out before I had qualified, it was decided that I should now become camp paymaster. This involved not only receiving our pay in bulk from the Nips and doling it out, but also handling the hospital central messing fund, which was keeping me busy. I had kept with my train party, for whom I was responsible; but with them now all being split up into various new wards, it didn't matter much where I went. Except to me.

In addition to the wards there was an administrative hut which housed the Force Commander and his staff and all of the doctors at one end, and the Nip Guards at the other. This hut was far less crowded, and so I suggested that I should move in and join the elite, and my request was granted. I had nearly three feet of shoulder space on the chung instead of just over twenty inches, and my cup seemed full.

The trauma of the hut-move subsided, and one could look around. Our main trouble was lack of water.

Water for the cook-house was brought in in barrels by lorry from the river, but the quantity was barely sufficient for cooking, and certainly left no margin for any other purposes. The ration was half a pint of tea with each of our three daily meals (the Nips were now including tea leaves with our rations, although of course with no milk or sugar), and so as well as constantly being thirsty, we had nothing for washing ourselves, our clothes or our dishes.

Little erections of groundsheets or waterproofs on small bamboo scaffoldings sprang up around the camp under the eaves of the hut roofs: but rain was now spasmodic, and with the attap being new such water as could be collected was dark brown and full of bits. Nevertheless, it was perfectly adequate for washing, albeit that we could collect nothing like enough of it. One worked on the conservative principle of using about a pint in a mess tin, soaking a little bit of cloth in it, and then wiping oneself down and drying oneself in the sun: but the time when I most regretted the water shortage was one dreadful night when I suffered a horrible calamity.

I still had worms and so had frequent recourse to the latrine. One night I was crouching in solitary splendour at about 3 a.m. Here, the latrine although of the same usual type, a long open trench with slats over the top, had an attap roof which kept the rain off but which also shut out nearly all of the faint moonlight.

Suddenly a fellow sufferer rushed out of the hut, and just managed to reach the first 'slot'. In the darkness he was unable to see, and not having time to adopt a proper crouching position, simply pointed his rump in the direction of the trench and let fly. He could not see that I was already in occupation of the first 'slot', and the worst of all possible fates overwhelmed me.

'Sorry', he muttered, which I felt in the circumstances to be a trifle inadequate: choking back the most horrible curses (only curses, mercifully, as I had just managed to dodge my head in time) I squelched oozily back to the hut to wash myself from the shoulders downwards in a mess-tinful of water which I perforce stole from a neighbouring catchment groundsheet, having none myself in reserve: and when I ate my breakfast from that same mess tin five hours later I first realized to the full what a blessing running tap water can be. We had no tap water.

At the cook-house water was stored in a row of huge chattis – large earthenware jars of the Ali Baba variety – but these held enough for only one meal at a time, and so there was no reserve should the lorry fail to arrive. This it did about once or twice a week, being of very doubtful vintage and liable to frequent breakdowns: the announcement which we came to dread was the mid-morning message that it had failed to come in, and that the midday meal would not be available until 5 o'clock, but there was at least some hope of a third meal, with a third half-pint of tea by around nine.

A little extra water came in by being bought off the natives through the fence. They brought it from the well in the nearby kampong, but advisedly would not part with their buckets. You could only buy it if you had your own bucket into which to tip it, and as only very few of us had buckets or petrol tins, that, more than availability, limited what could come into the camp. The fortunate few with buckets did an easy trade hawking it around the wards, having themselves already boiled it and made it fit for drinking.

As it was available from the kampong well, we approached the Nips, and almost to our surprise they were co-operative. They agreed that we could send out an organized party each day under a Nip Guard, and they placed no limit on the numbers going. We had an 'official' cook-house party, but individuals could go as well. It meant half a mile either way, and then a wait in the queue of up to two hours (the cook-house party rightly being given priority), but there was nothing much else to do anyway, and water was such a precious commodity that it was well worth it. That brought in by the cook-house party enabled us to give the malaria and dysentery patients (who were the most dehydrated) two pints of tea a day against the official ration of only a pint and a half: and if you are in the grip of fever and in the tropics, an extra half pint does not come amiss.

The 'private hawkers' continued to do a good trade, and a number of other men, who hadn't got buckets, devised other means of doing business. From smallish vessels they would sell you hot sweet coffee, or they would provide ready-boiled or fried eggs. One man came around offering to boil your own eggs for you for one cent, or to fry them for you for two and a half cents which included the cost of the oil. If you couldn't yourself move down from your chung, this was a godsend.

Yet others, trying to earn an honest copper, would come round offering to darn your socks, grease your boots, or de-scale and polish your mess tin, whilst two energetic Dutchmen (one whole group of H Force were Dutch prisoners from Java), went round with a hatchet and a mallet and for fifteen cents would take all the bamboos off your stretch of chung, split them into narrower and springier lengths, shave off all the knobbly bits, and remake them into a smoother, more comfortable, bed.

Private enterprise was helping life to become more tolerable for the few, but the rest of us were returning to civilization in any case.

Ulcers were on the increase, but the Nips were now persuaded to find us some chloroform, and the Australian Major, Kevin, could now really get to work. As soon as the chloroform arrived he started operating, although in somewhat crude conditions. He had two planks raised on boxes next to the prime ulcer ward, and there, stripped to the waist and wearing a pair of gym shoes, he did his stuff. His anaesthetist stood at one end, holding the chloroform bottle in one hand and his hat, above the bottle, in the other, to prevent evaporation; whilst two orderlies stood by waving large fly swats to keep the blue-bottles away from the succulent putrefaction. Meanwhile Kevin hacked away, dropping the rotting flesh into a petol tin.

Within only a week, he had a proper operating theatre rigged up – a little fly-proof tent with a mosquito net acquired from a dead man's kit – and he could carry on without attendant fly swatters. Fortunately for me, he didn't have to 'carry-on' on me.

He had threatened me. My ulcer was getting worse, and he had told me that unless I kept my leg up and stopped walking about, he would have to take my leg off. He gave me three weeks, and said that unless it had improved by then, he would have no option. He now had some iodine, and the risk of gangrene had diminished – but my lucky streak continued.

I learnt that amongst the milling crowd of Thai villagers who came to trade with us through the fence, there was a man who had some drugs for sale. They had no doubt been stolen from the Japanese, but as they were British Red Cross supplies it was the Japanese who had stolen them in the first place, and so I had no qualms about 'dealing in stolen goods'. One of the lines which he had was M & B tablets. I have no medical knowledge, but to the layman M & B was the forerunner of penicillin (which at that time was not in circulation), and it cleared up pus. It could clear up ulcers.

He was charging twenty-five ticals for two tablets, but the doctor beside whom I was now sleeping told me that two would be just a waste of money, and that I should need at least sixteen – eight doses. Sixteen would cost two hundred ticals, and I hadn't got two hundred ticals nor any sum near it.

Another little bit of private enterprise had sprung up within the camp. There were men who had accumulated money, but could no longer use it to buy valuables from other prisoners, as there were no more valuables to buy. They would sell you ticals, which you could use immediately, for undated UK cheques which they could encash after the war. They were charging one pound per tical, which might seem to be horrendously exorbitant, but they ran the very real risk of never eventually collecting, either because you had immorally stopped the cheque, or because you had simply died and the account had been closed.

I got in touch with a money broker, and said that I wanted two hundred ticals. He had got them, and asked for my cheque, whereupon trouble arose.

He was familiar with the big five – Barclays, the National Provincial, the Midland, Lloyds, and the Westminster – but I banked with and had the remnants of a Coutts cheque book. He had never heard of Coutts, but although I assured him that they indeed existed and were quite respectable (being the bankers to the Royal Family), he would only deal at a fifty per cent discount, charging me two pounds per tical. Wounding although it may be to the *amour propre* of Coutts, I settled. I gave him a cheque for four hundred pounds, collected my two hundred ticals, and that afternoon I got my sixteen M & B tablets. We didn't just swallow them in the normal manner – we ground them up and applied the powder direct to the affected area, which was apparently more economical of their capabilities – but it *worked*. Within a fortnight my ulcer was on the mend and was healing, and Kevin reprieved my leg.

Four hundred pounds for sixteen M & B tablets may sound excessive. Four hundred pounds to save the amputation of your leg is very, very cheap. The cheque was duly presented for payment at my bank after the war, and I made no attempt to stop it and let it be paid gladly. Without those two hundred ticals and those resultant sixteen M & B tablets, I shouldn't be trotting around on two legs today.

My mentor over this was a Doctor Murphy, who slept on the chung next to me. He was not from H Force, but from one of the earlier parties, and his present job was to be in medical charge of the adjoining coolie camp. 'In charge' was an exaggeration. He was allowed in for one visit a day, accompanied by one Administrative Officer and two medical orderlies. We got quite friendly, and we chatted each evening about his day's experiences.

They were almost unbelievable.

Each day, he was given his allocation of 'drugs'. There were over 2,000 coolies in the camp, and the Japs gave him one bottle of iodine with which to cope with over 1,000 ulcers, one bottle of quinine to cope with well over 1,000 malaria patients, and one bottle of bicarbonate of soda, which did not claim to cure, but was meant to alleviate the discomfort of gonorrhoea, from which the coolies were suffering badly; we were not, not having had the same opportunities as the coolies.

Worst of all were their 'dysentery wards'. There were two of them, although there had originally only been one. They were at the far end of the camp, and although outwardly similar in appearance to the others – two sloping roofs going down to the floor on either side – inside they were different. Instead of the basic solid floor in the middle, the middle had been dug out into a large trench going through the entire length of the hut: this was a latrine. The Japs argued that the occupants of the hut could not make it to the outside latrines, and that it was more convenient for them to have the latrines handy. They therefore slept adjacent to their latrines, smelly or not.

The central latrine had another feature. It had no slats, and so would-be users merely had to crouch over the sides. If the user slipped backwards, bad luck. There were quite a few bodies in the central latrine, and nobody particularly relished the task of fishing them out. They stayed there. Once a day, a fatigue party went around the hut collecting the corpses of those who had died within the past twenty-four hours, the bodies being taken out and buried in a single 'one day's pit'. The spare spaces on the chungs in the hut were rapidly filled with victims from other huts who had developed the disease.

The Japanese reacted with their customary chilling logic. Men transferred to the dysentery huts were almost certainly going to die, and so why waste precious resources on them? They cut off the rations. Food was precious, but so was water, which had to be brought into the camp as well as wood to fuel the boilers to boil the water and make it 'safe for drinking'. They simply cut off the water ration as well as the food.

Murphy protested violently, and to his surprise the Japs not only listened to him but agreed to a compromise. The dysentery wards could continue to have a water ration, but it would be water straight out of the well and not boiled and so 'safe for drinking'. It might be contaminated, but so what? They were going to die anyway, and it could meanwhile spare them the added agony of thirst. The water ration was restored, thanks entirely to Doctor Murphy.

He could do nothing about having the bodies cleared from the central latrines. The coolie fatigue squads did not want to do it. The Japs suggested to Murphy that he might like to bring in British prisoners to do it, but he did not think that he would get many volunteers. The bodies remained, floating in the latrines. If, as a victim, you found yourself crouching willy-nilly over the face of your erstwhile best friend, you had no option but to defecate upon him, praying only that you might not slip over the edge and join him in drowning in a less than salubrious way.

We had latrine troubles of our own. There was not much space between or behind our huts, and we were running out of space to dig more trenches. We asked the Japs if we could dig new trenches on the other side of the railway. They replied that they could not have our troops running across the railway ad lib, but they had a suggestion. We could send an organized party, under supervision, over the railway to dig a new pit, and then, each day, we could lay on a fatigue party to scoop up the contents of our present latrine in buckets and carry them over to the new pit. Not the nicest of jobs, but the idea appeared to tickle the fancy of our captors, and they insisted upon it being done.

Little more happened to H Force, as such, over the next couple of months. We had been told, early on, that this was a 'recuperation camp', with no working parties other than for looking after ourselves – bringing in water and firewood – and that once we had recuperated (i.e. that once all of those already dying had obligingly reduced our numbers) we were going to be shipped back to Singapore. The balance of H Force trickled in, including even that last-minute working party demanded before we left Canu. They had gone further up-country, and had been made to work extremely long hours; but they had been given surprisingly generous rations, and had suffered very few casualties, emphasizing that our troubles were now less related to disease than to starvation.

Pressure on bed space eased: although new captives were coming in, they were outnumbered by men dying, and leaving more room in the huts. Life was getting better.

Bed space pressure was even more relieved. So many coolies had died that the Japs moved the fence, separating the two camps, up two notches, giving them four fewer huts (two on each side) and us four more. We were a little hesitant about fumigation and disinfection, but the answer was comparatively simple – we used the new huts as dysentery wards.

As well as the remnants of H Force, we had small sporadic intakes of other camps, which were being closed down, mainly from the remnants of F Force.

F Force had had a far worse time then we had. Seven thousand strong at the outset, they had been forced to march 190 to 210 miles up into the jungle; H Force having been faced with only less than 100 miles. F Force had been 'fitter' than we, the cream of the best which Changi could manage, whereas the subsequent 3,000 for H Force had been mustered from the dregs. Nevertheless, of F Force's original 7,000, no fewer than 2,000 had either fallen by the wayside or had died on their march up. Their remnants were now being withdrawn, not to Kamburi, but to Tamarkand Bridge. There had been about 4,000 survivors out of their original 7,000, but no fewer than 46 died on the two-day train journey down, and another 186 died within three weeks of arrival.

On their way up, F Force had been put through wholly unnecessary and avoidable hell. Their designated working area was around Three Pagoda Pass, on the Thailand-Burma border some 200 miles up-country west of Bampong, whereas H Force was to follow only some 100 miles up-country around Canu. The stretch in between, less hilly and needing a more level track bed with fewer cuttings and embankments, was being worked by the Thai labour force, who were already there.

The parties of F Force were made to use the existing Thai camps as staging posts on their march: but the Thais had already got cholera. Our F Force Party Commanders had protested with all their might pleading that our men should bypass the camps and preferably just sleep in the open in the jungle – but the Nips would have none of it. The plan said that they would stage at the Thai camps, the rice rations had already been dumped there, and into the Thai camps our men would go, with the hideous result that by the time they reached Three Pagoda Pass, every single one of the thirteen truck-parties which made up F Force was itself infected with cholera.

Blind adherence to the plan was exemplified by an occasion when one party found a Nip Medical Officer at Tarso, and persuaded him to go through their ranks and vet some very sick men. The Nip, by no means soft hearted, weeded out thirty-six men, and told the column Guard Commander to leave them behind. The Guard Commander, a Corporal, had retorted that his orders were that all men had got to march on, and march on they would. He, a Corporal, was not going to be overruled by a mere Medical Captain. When the British CO protested, he was bashed over the head and the interpreter was properly beaten up. The Corporal responded to the protests of our own MO (a Major) with such violence that he broke his wrist (the MO's – not his own). The thirty-six joined the night's march, but it is scarcely surprising that not one of them made it to the border.

As batches were brought across from Tamarkand Bridge to Kamburi, pressure on bed spaces again made itself felt: but then suddenly we got a demand from the Nips for a working party of 600 fit men. We hadn't got 600 who were as yet really fit; but the Nips told us to produce the 600 fittest that we had got, and off they went on a train. To our mild surprise, the train went off eastwards towards Bampong, rather than back up-country: but we had long ceased to speculate on what might happen to us. The only effect upon those of us who remained was that we had fewer fit men left for water carrying, latrine emptying, and so on. Men who had been 'excused from heavy duties' now had to take their turns.

The going of the 600 had again relieved the pressure on bed spaces, and there was the gradual exodus of the dead: but the death rate was now slowing down, and we relapsed into a state of just going on from day to day. And then the magic announcement was made. We were to stand by for evacuation to Singapore.

We got ourselves organized into truck-loads, and stood by all next day – and the next – and the next. The third day was our monthly pay day, and it was evident that the Japs were in earnest about the impending move: they paid us in Malay dollars instead of in Thai ticals. This brought us momentary encouragement, but it shortly brought us problems.

It was a full four weeks before we eventually moved, in spite of numerous false alarms when we were told 'Go tomorrow', and in the meantime the Thai contractor running the official canteen, as well as the locals trading through the perimeter, wouldn't touch dollars with a barge-pole. They wanted ticals, and in the absence of ticals our supplies of eggs and bananas dried up completely. We asked the Nips to change our money back, but they resolutely refused, each time saying 'Go tomorrow'.

15   Changi Gaol

'Tomorrow' eventually arrived, and one train-load went off. I was on train number 2, and although expecting a wait of several further days, we went off on day two.

The train was made up of the solid rice trucks similar to those in which we had come up from Singapore rather than the open trucks by now more familiar on our part of the line; as we clambered aboard we found that there was even rush matting on the floors.

The rush matting was thrown out within the hour. It was alive with lice (with which few of us had been troubled before) and they troubled us now with a vengeance. There were plenty of them to go round, and so we all got our share: even when we threw the matting out, the lice stayed with us. During the six day journey we were not allowed off even once to wash under the engine water towers, and the lice had no doubt received the Divine instruction 'Go forth and multiply' which they obeyed delightedly.

It was not a happy journey. Apart from the lice, which itched abominably, we only got one meal a day, starting on our second day (we had each brought a mess-tinful of cooked rice to see us through the first day), save for one glorious day when we were already over the border out of Thailand and back into Malaya, and we got two meals: once into Malaya we appreciated why the Thais had refused dollars and demanded ticals.

Prices had rocketed. Eggs, five cents each or sometimes three for ten cents on the way up, were now sixty cents each or two for a dollar. Bananas were rare, although at one small village halt there was a table laid out with some exceedingly tempting ready-cooked banana fritters, done up like pounds of sausages six at a time in cellophane. It was only just as we were about to move off that this superb display of hygiene received a bit of a shock. A cockerel was walking daintily along the table, pecking at the packages and trying to get through the cellophane. A small native boy ran up, clapping: in the confusion, the cockerel kicked several packets down onto the churned-up mud ground, where they burst, spilling out the fritters.

The small boy picked them out of the black, oozy, smelly mud, wiped them off on the end of his sarong, covered them again in the cellophane, and put the packages back amongst the others on the table.

That village had something to sell. On the way up, at every halt we had been surrounded by villagers eager to sell us fruit, eggs, or whatever. Now, on the way back, all that we usually met were small groups of pathetic little pot-bellied youngsters, obviously on the borderline of starvation, holding out their sarongs to try to beg rice off *us*. Malaya was not what it had been.

Branch lines from the main railway, and even sidings at major halts, had been torn up, the rails themselves having gone up-country to supply the accursed Bangkok-Moulmein link. Rubber plantations through which the railway passed were neglected and overgrown as the coolies who had previously worked them had been siphoned off and sent up-country on the working parties; whilst even the largest stations were in a state of appalling neglect, obviously with no cleaning or maintenance and in a state of filth which only the Japanese could tolerate let alone supervise.

Malaya was definitely running down.

One small, but to me significant, incident stands out on that journey.

In our truck, we had twenty-five men – three officers and the rest other ranks. One of the officers was a Major Pery Standish, a friend of mine, and he had been sitting in the open door with his legs dangling out. We passed a signal or some warning sign which was nearer the truck than usual, and it caught his foot very, very painfully. We had no MO in the truck, but at the next stop I jumped down and went back several trucks looking for a man called Elze.

Elze was a Dutch-Javanese-Jew, as black as the night – but if you had one per cent of Dutch blood you counted, in the Dutch Army, as 'Dutch', and he was therefore one of our party. I had seen him operating up at Kamburi. He had a gift of hypnotism, but he was very strict about using it. He refused point blank to join concert parties or to use it for entertaining, saying that it was a gift from God to be used only on God's work. Up at Kamburi he would go into the ulcer wards and see a man with a large ulcer on his knee, who had his leg drawn up and hadn't been able to straighten it for days, let alone get a night's sleep. Elze would fix him with a gaze (he had large and most penetrating eyes) and start intoning 'Your pain is going away. Straighten your leg. Go to sleep.' And the man would close his eyes, straighten his leg, and *go* to sleep. I saw it happen several times, and I *believed* in him. The regular Medical Officers hated him – he was not part of the 'Qualified Establishment' and was therefore a 'quack' – but it was any port in a storm, and I went down and he agreed to come back to our truck.

Pery had never seen him in operation in the ulcer wards and was sceptical. 'This is wholly physical, not mental', he said.

'Would you like me to give you a little demonstration?' asked Elze.

'Can't do any harm, I suppose', replied Pery somewhat ungraciously.

'You have a pencil in your breast pocket', said Elze. 'Put it down on the floor beside you'. Pery did. 'Now pick it up,' said Elze. Pery tried. He put out a casual hand and gripped the pencil – but it didn't move. He gripped it more tightly, but it wouldn't budge. He tugged at it, tried to wriggle it around, and tugged and tugged again. It was though it was welded to the floor.

'Now try again', said Elze. Pery almost fell backwards as it came up perfectly normally. 'Convinced?' asked Elze. 'Shall we try your foot now?' He not only tried, but he *did* it. The train was already on the move again by now, but we got Elze back to his own truck at the next stop: he now had two believers – Pery and me – in his uncanny powers. They were to serve me later.

The train pulled itself together and rattled at a fair speed through the final stretch of Johore: having gone over the now repaired causeway onto the Island, we pulled into Singapore Station, darkish and ill-lit, at half past eight.

There was a convoy of lorries waiting for us. We spent only an hour or so getting out and being counted, truck-load by truck-load, and then we were loaded up into the lorries. To our surprise, we were not driven off eastwards towards Changi, but were driven northwards.

We came to Sime Road. On one side of the road was the old golf course, still looking impeccable. On the other side of the road was the former British Advanced Headquarters. This had been built just before the war, and they had not stinted on expense. It only consisted of wooden huts, but they were proper huts with real roofs rather than just attap; they had verandahs, they had concrete floors, and they had real doors rather than just open gaps. The site was an undulating collection of little hills and valleys, and instead of the huts being built in long uninteresting rows, they were dotted around all over the place, mostly on little hillock tops. Proper concrete paths connected them all up. Miraculously, the camp had not been damaged either in the bombing or in the fighting.

We went through the gateway in the perimeter fence almost in wonderment: but there was another surprise awaiting us. We were greeted by some fit and healthy looking prisoners, who were none other than that first party of our own people who had left Kamburi several weeks earlier. At the time we had assumed that they were going back up-country for more work on the railway, and had grumbled and groused about not having *got* 600 fit men. We had been slightly puzzled to see their train move off in the direction of Bampong rather than going west-wards, but it now transpired that they had been brought down to Sime Road to get the camp ready for the rest of us! The camp had not been in use for some time, but in the last four weeks the working party had cleared up all the litter, mown all the grass between the huts, checked the water and the electricity, and so on.

The first thing was a meal. It had been cooked for us by the working party, and although they had been told to expect us some hours earlier, it had been kept hot and we fell to immediately. It was terrific. The ration scale in the camp was the full one pound, uncooked, a day, which was by now little more than a memory: but even better it consisted of only two-thirds rice and one-third soya beans – far more nutritious than rice and rich in fat, protein, and above all vitamin B. And we were told that in future we should be getting three meals a day. This is why the working party looked fat and fit, whilst we looked thin and hungry.

We ate our rice and beans, with a yam stew and a pint of hot tea; and then before stretching out on the beautiful smooth concrete floor, I experienced the wonderful sensation of standing under a real mains tap and having a shower. Actually, I couldn't stand up, as the tap was only about 3 feet off the ground: but I curled myself up into a ball, and it was the nearest thing to Heaven which I can ever recollect.

For eight months running water had been one of our rosiest dreams: and I personally not only had a 'shower' before bedding down for the night, but also one during the night, when the lice were biting particularly badly, and I got up and had another one. The following morning, I washed all of my clothes and my blanket and spread them out in the sun to dry, running around happily naked meanwhile.

It didn't dispose of quite all of the lice, but it shook them badly. I repeated the process each day, and after only three or four days I was completely louse free. If you take running water for granted – don't. It is one of the most precious boons of civilization.

For four days we were kept within a short radius of our huts, and not allowed to wander freely all over the camp. We were then given a medical inspection, and were 'medically categorized'. Once this had been done, we were moved to other huts all over the camp, according to our 'categories'. For the first time in our prisoner of war existence officers and men were separated – up until now we had all been in it together. And furthermore, for the first time all nationalities were mixed together – previously we had been kept in batches – huts or even half-huts – as British, Australian, or Dutch. I was now put in charge of a hut containing eighty-five officers – twenty Australians, fifteen Dutch, a sprinkling of Americans, and the rest British. It worked like a dream – there was far less bickering, far less jealousy on the grounds of 'their hut has got far more headroom on the bed spaces than we have', and international co-operation really worked.

We were not cut off from the other ranks – we were in separate huts, but we could wander around freely all day and keep in touch with them.

Within two months I had put on two stone in weight, thanks largely to the soya beans (which nevertheless played dramatic havoc with one's bowels): but I was running into trouble. My leg ulcer had healed, thanks to my M & B tablets, but my left big toe had gone septic. They bathed it with salt water for a while, but instead of it clearing up it got worse, and I was told that it would not improve whilst the nail was still growing.

It would be no good simply yanking the nail out, leaving the nail bed to go on growing a new nail, and so I was told that the only answer was to chop off the first joint of my toe, which would include the nail bed. I was not keen, but then I was not keen on what I had got already.

They had rigged up a well-organized, if not well-equipped, hospital, covering several huts; and in I went. They had very very few anaesthetics, reserved only for very serious cases. The best they could do for me by way of anaesthetics was one burly Australian medical orderly lying across my ribs to stop me getting up, with another equally strong character lying across my knees to keep my legs still. The surgeon started on my toe, and mercifully I passed out, and needed no further anaesthetics.

The Spanish Inquisition boys knew their stuff. It is surprising how many little nerves congregate in the thumbs and the big toes, and when they invented thumb screws they knew what they were doing. When I came to, back in a ward, I spent a whole day tossing around in the worst pain that I can remember. So bad was I that they gave me a shot of their precious morphine, but it made no difference. I eventually had an idea, and asked if they could find Elze for me. They could – he was in one of the wards himself – and he was with me very shortly.

We recognized one another, and I had no need of a 'demonstration'. I trusted him. He held his hands a few inches above my knee (I was lying down) and drew his hands down above my shins to my feet. When he got there, he wrung and shook his hands and said 'I'm drawing the pain down from your body and throwing it onto the floor'. That sounds absolutely ridiculous, but he was *doing* it. He was trembling and sweating, and he did it several times more – and the pain completely went out of my toe.

I slept all night, and when I awoke in the morning there was still no pain. But I needed to use a bed pan, and as soon as I did, the spell was broken and the pain raged up again. I asked the orderly to get Elze again, but he was away for a good ten minutes. When he came back he said 'I'm sorry, Sir. He was only in the next ward, but he died overnight – he had black-water fever'. I must have been his last patient, but I shall forever remember him – and ridiculous although 'I am throwing your pain onto the floor' may sound, nothing will ever convince me that there isn't a lot in hypnotism.

We had five months in this heavenly camp, and realized that it couldn't last: and it didn't. We received orders that we were to move back to Changi, but not into our original camps but into the gaol.

Right from the beginning, the Nips had used the gaol at Changi for the civilian internees – civilians who had not managed to get away before Singapore fell, but were not in the armed forces and were not therefore prisoners of war. A cheerless pile of grey concrete, it stood about 2 miles south of the main Changi complex, to the right of the only main road leading in.

It had been built only a few years before the war, and was modelled, so we were told, on America's Sing-Sing: a gaunt square of a 20-foot wall, with watch towers, searchlights, and machine gun posts at each corner, a road inside the main wall and then another 12-foot wall housing the cell blocks, two each comprising 240 cells, plus the punishment block and the administrative block. Not a pretty edifice.

There were about 300 women and children, but these were rigorously segregated from the men; and no contact even between husbands and wives was permitted. By putting the men onto such jobs as the cleaning of the outside drains around the women's block, occasional brief contacts were achieved: but generally speaking the lives of all of them had been pretty dreary, and it wasn't much fun for the children. At any event, they had not been unduly overcrowded.

The Nips now announced that the internees were to be moved down to Sime Road, 'where they could all be together', and that we were to go up to Changi and take their places in the gaol.

We received this news with mixed feelings. It would obviously be nice for the internees, particularly for the women and children, but as there were far more of us than there were of them, the gaol was going to be a bit overcrowded. However, for children cooped up in a particularly grim gaol for well over two years, it would seem a miracle come true, and we raised no objections with the Nips on the grounds of overcrowding lest they called the transfers off.

On the whole, the internees had not done too badly. Their only trouble (apart from the customary semi-starvation, disease, and isolation) had come on 10 October in the previous year – a date remembered as 'the double tenth' from the Chinese festival falling on that date, when the Nips discovered their radio receiver and kicked up hell.

There was more to it than just the wireless. The men, led by the Bishop of Singapore, had organized a chain of contact with the Chinese outside for smuggling food into the camp. A lorry on its way in, one day, was searched, a parcel discovered, and when the Kempi were called in the fat was in the fire.

All of the internees, men, women, and children, were turned out and kept standing in the main courtyard for twenty-four hours without food or water under the broiling sun and through the chill of the night whilst the Kempi went through the whole place with a fine-tooth comb. In a concrete gaol there were not the same facilities for concealment as there were in the POW camps; and the Kempi unearthed not only the radio but also lists of their Chinese contacts with what they were owed and so forth.

Leaping to the conclusion that a plot for widespread resistance, sabotage, and escaping was being secretly organized, the Kempi went wild, and hauled off a number of men, including the Bishop, and several women to their Outram Road headquarters. There they went through the usual routines to 'extract information' – even the Bishop being brutally beaten up – and although during the next six months they were let out in dribs and drabs, fifteen of them died and a number of others were shattered men when they returned.

So much for the civilians, but when the transfers took place we found that Changi had changed dramatically since we had left it over a year ago. The erstwhile dream haven of no work, running water, electric light and regular news bulletins which had figured so largely in our longings up-country, had now lost much of its savour. The Nips were building a large airfield, and guess who was going to help with the digging and the levelling? Right first time – we were. Having had some months of 'rest and rehabilitation' at Sime Road, we were now expected to be fit and healthy and ready to move mountains – or if not mountains, at least a fair-sized hill. The central runway was long enough and level enough, but very narrow, and was flanked on one side by a hill, and on the other side by a swamp. The idea was to dig out the hill and tip it into the swamp, getting a nice broad level runway. The Nips did not have bulldozers or levellers or anything sophisticated like that: but as an alternative they had gangs of POWs with picks and shovels demolishing the hill, and other gangs carrying the spoil in wicker baskets across the meagre runway and tipping it into the swamp. Slow, but effective. After all, the ancient Egyptians didn't have much else other than slave labour when they built the pyramids, did they?

That, however, was for our future rather than our

immediacy. The gaol was not empty, but had already been almost filled by the former occupants of the old POW camps in Changi, which camps were now being evacuated to make way for the airfield. When we arrived, we were told that there were still some attap huts in the old camps, and we were to go and get them and re-erect them on the outskirts of the gaol. We did our best, but they were now old and rickety, the dry attap roofing crumbling if touched. We took three weeks, but finally got them transferred to their new sites, with cannibalized roofs to make a few tolerably watertight. In one of them, I was destined to spend the rest of the year until the B 29s got busy.

Life became routine. Work on the airfield was not easy, but one came back to a dry billet, running water to wash in and wash one's clothes in, and we soon had gardens planted with very quick-growing greenstuff with which to supplement our rations. It was very different from Thailand.

The Nips not only permitted, but encouraged us to run the vegetable garden, with 500 men a day, not fit for airfield duties, doing a few hours at a time. On one grisly occasion they even 'protected' our garden.

A Chinaman had been caught stealing. He was beaten up, and then his hands were tied in the small of his back with a wire, the end of which was brought up and looped around his throat. Another wire (thin, flexible wire) was then looped around his neck in a noose, and the end of this was then hung up on the doorpost of the tool shed, in such a way that when he stood on tip-toe he was able to breathe – but if he sagged, the wire would cut in, draw tight, and strangle him. To complete the picture, the Nips then got a third piece of wire, looped it around his neck, and on the end suspended the jack from a lorry, dangling loosely on the level of his shins – and every Nip who went by gave the pendulum a swing so that it swung about and battered his shins to a bruised, bloody pulp.

For two days and two nights – such were his powers of resistance and his will to live – he managed to stay on his toes: but at last exhaustion and the weight of the jack to say nothing of the ghastly state of his legs proved too much. He sagged, and of course he died: the Nips left his body hanging there for two more days *pour encourager les autres*.

They did something perhaps even more horrible to another thief. In this case, by the time that we arrived it was all over, but it wasn't difficult to reconstruct what had happened. From the weals on his body and limbs the Nips had evidently given him the usual preliminary beating up: then they had crammed his mouth with coarse salt, and sewn his lips together with a bootlace.

The salt, as intended, had made him want to vomit, and this in turn had led him uncontrollably to try to open his mouth. There he had writhed, alternately vomiting, straining and tearing his lips to agonizing shreds against the bootlace, swallowing his vomit perforce and then vomiting over and over again. The Nips had evidently eventually tired of this entertainment, and putting a rope around his neck had strung him up and left him to strangle slowly: there we found the corpse next morning, still swinging from the branch of a tree, with the pitiful heap of three stolen melons lying on the ground beside him.

The Nips were far, far worse in their treament of the local natives than they were in their treatment of us; but we still feared our ultimate fate.

Time dragged. We had, of course, a camp radio, and all the indications were that the Allies were gradually winning the war. We heard of the gradual take-over of Burma, but not knowing the conditions, we felt that the 14th Army was taking a long, long time. The Allied Commander was now Lord Louis Mountbatten, and as time dragged on he became known to us as 'Lingering Louis'; a terrible fear gripped us that we might eventually be freed not by the British but by the Americans, who seemed to be doing rather well in the Pacific.

Our Nip Camp Commander was much better behaved than our Commanders up in Thailand had been. Although frequently drunk, and difficult to approach when the hangovers were troubling him, he was nevertheless occasionally approachable and made a real effort to put some curb on his minions. Whether or not he had seen the light and was making sure that no rope would get around his neck after the war was over and a War Crimes Tribunal might be looking at his record doesn't really matter. Suffice it to say that he was almost human, and on several occasions he even supported us against the Engineers who were in charge of the airfield.

Certainly he had no illusions about who was winning the war, albeit that the radio broadcasts from either side were heavily biased, boasting of successes whilst minimizing, if mentioning at all, reverses. And to him was attributed the famous retort when our own CO approached him and asked him what the latest news was. 'There are only two radios on Singapore Island capable of listening both to the BBC and to Nippon Radio', he retorted. 'One is at Japanese Headquarters, and they won't tell me. The other one is yours, and you won't tell me either'. Whether or not he did in fact make that remark, he without a doubt knew that we *were* running a set – but he had as much to fear personally from the Kempi for not having 'discovered' it as we had ourselves.

The really big news came after just a year. The BBC announced that a new type of bomb had been dropped on the Japanese mainland on a town called Hiroshima. Radio Nippon ordered everyone to stand by for an important announcement from the Emperor. The news was not allowed out to the camp in general for fear that everyone would look too jubilant: but shortly Nagasaki got its visitation as well, and the Emperor announced the cessation of hostilities and unconditional surrender. Still we suppressed the news, as it was by no means certain that outlying Jap armies, such as that in Malaya, might not disobey and would attempt to fight on – and if they did, we had little doubt that in 'fighting to the death' they would take their prisoners (us) with them.

They did not, but it was over a week before our Nip Camp Commander called our own CO into his office and said 'The war is over. Nippon has surrendered' and he handed over his sword. The war was indeed over, thanks

to those two glorious little bombs, which certainly saved
the lives of thousands upon thousands of prisoners.

Epilogue

'Forgive and forget' is a well-known Christian ethic.

Many of our chief tormentors – Musso, The Bull, and even Oswald – were duly hanged in 1946 after trial by the War Crimes Tribunal. The hundreds of others are now in their sixties or seventies or probably dead.

The other ethic is that 'the crimes of the fathers shall be visited upon their children and their children's children'. Rubbish. We have a new generation of Japs now, who were in no way responsible for what their fathers and grandfathers did half a century ago. I should like to be friends with them, and I will certainly trade with them. I have a Japanese camera, a Japanese video, a Japanese Hi-Fi and I even drive a Japanese car. There is nothing for me to 'forgive' the present blameless generation.

'Forgetting' is entirely different. I shall never forget the hundreds of my friends who were driven to their deaths and whose bodies were left to rot in those ghastly jungles of Siam. Forgive – yes: there are few left to forgive. Forget – no. Maybe I'm not a very good Christian. I cannot observe the overall ethic.

Index

Index